A Critical Reading of the Development of Raimon Panikkar's Thought on the Trinity

Camilia Gangasingh MacPherson

University Press of America, Inc.
Lanham • New York • London

Copyright © 1996 by
University Press of America,® Inc.
4720 Boston Way
Lanham, Maryland 20706

3 Henrietta Street
London, WC2E 8LU England

Library of Congress Cataloging-in-Publication Data

MacPherson, Camilia Gangasingh.
A critical reading of the development of Raimon Panikkar's thought on
the Trinity / Camilia Gangasingh MacPherson.
p.   cm.
1. Trinity--History of doctrines--20th century. 2. Christianity and
other religions--History of doctrines--20th century. 3. Panikkar,
Raimundo, 1918- I. Title.
BT109.M3   1996   231'.044'092--dc20   96-43443   CIP

ISBN 0-7618-0183-9 (cloth: alk. ppr.)
ISBN 0-7618-0184-7 (pbk: alk. ppr.)

⊖™The paper used in this publication meets the minimum
requirements of American National Standard for information
Sciences—Permanence of Paper for Printed Library Materials,
ANSI Z39.48—1984

To my children

David

Laura-Marie

Anne-Marie

Contents

Outline of the Life of
Raimon Panikkar (1918-)

1918   Born in Barcelona, Spain, November 3rd
1946   Received doctorate in philosophy (University of Madrid).
        Ordained Roman Catholic Priest
1955   Went to India in search of cultural roots and to study Indian
        philosophy and religion
1958   Received doctorate in chemistry (University of Madrid)
1961   A "Founding Father" of the Castelli Conferences on
        Hermeneutics, University of Rome. Received doctorate in
        theology (Lateran University, Rome)
1967   Went to United States of America (while retaining contact with
        the East)
1967-71 Visiting Professor of Comparative Religion at the Center for
        the Study of World Religions, Harvard University
1971-87 Professor of Comparative Philosophy and History of Religions,
        Department of Religious Studies of the University of California,
        Santa Barbara. Since 1987 Professor Emeritus of the University
        of California, Santa Barbara
1989   Gave the Gifford Lectures at the University of Edinburgh
1991   Gave the Warren Lecture at the University of Tulsa and Cardinal
        Bellarmine Lecture at St. Louis University.
1992   Lives quietly in Tavertet, Spain. Continues contact with the
        East. He is a citizen of India.

Preface

My Hindu father and Moslem mother have afforded me fertile ground for appreciating the world religions. My travels to Africa, Asia, the Middle East and Europe as well as my deep love for Buddhism further enriched my appreciation, respect and even devotion to the world religions. I am proud of being a Roman Catholic because of its rich heritage and openness to the universal expression of the Triune God. This has been for me ground on which I can stand and grow in my faith. Although I have worshipped in temples and mosques and continue to do so, I have found anchorage and love in Christ who has awakened in me the ability to recognize and give praise to the Triune God in numerous and universal expressions. Working as a Lay Pastoral Associate in a multicultural parish in Toronto for several years further enhanced my appreciation for God's universal expression.

Radical thinkers like Paul Knitter and Raimundo Panikkar have upset my Roman Catholic Theological equilibrium enabling me to rethink the Trinity and to recognize my stutterings of the written Word. Their friendship is treasured. Professor Dale Schlitt's courses on the world religions inspired within me questions I had never asked before. Professor Charles Amico, my teacher, mentor and friend since 1977, has kept me in safe waters as well as constantly exploring new rivers and sometimes new oceans. Professor James Pambrun, Professor Claude Champagne, Professor Provencher and the late Professor A.L. Basham provided invaluable assistance in the writing of this work.

The staffs of St. Paul's University Library (Ottawa, Ont.), Christ the King Seminary Library (East Aurora, N.Y.) and St. Augustine Seminary Library (Toronto, Ont.) were of immense assistance.

Introduction

Raimundo Panikkar's[1] concept of Trinity as it has evolved over the years contains important elements in furthering dialogue between Christianity and the other world religions, in particular Hinduism and Buddhism. The aim of this study is to show that there is a development in Panikkar's thought on the Trinity. It will be noted that there is basically an earlier Panikkar and a later Panikkar in relation to the Trinity. The earlier Panikkar wrestles with the problem of the experience of the Trinity from a Christian perspective within the depths of the human person in the Advaita tradition of Hinduism as well as from the perspective of the universality of the trinitarian experience among the world religions. The later Panikkar struggles with the same problem of the universality of the trinitarian experience as well as with the depth-experience of the Trinity within the individual but breaks out of the moulds of history and organized religions and locates the Trinity universally and within the depths of the human person in a way that barely resembles any religious categories.

Panikkar's main dialogue partner is the Advaita Vedanta tradition as he develops his concept of Trinity. He searches for the Trinity within the Advaita Vedanta School of Hinduism. Although he proceeds to a further concept of Trinity that will embrace all religions, he never lets go of the basic tenets of the Advaita Vedanta tradition. It becomes the current that sweeps him even beyond the world religions to the realm of the secular sphere without his ever letting go of the Advaitin tenet of Atman (innermost Self) equalling Braham (God).

The outline of this work is as follows. Chapter I will be divided into three sections. Section A will examine the context in which Panikkar develops his ideas on the Trinity. It will sketch his biography in order to show how it affects his trinitarian thought. It will then examine briefly the period of theological transition and turmoil out of which his ideas emerge. The last part of section A will point out that during the period in which Panikkar develops his trinitarian theology there is a lack of an adequate theology of religion. Section B will focus on Panikkar's methodology, namely, his general methodology in the light of the formative factors of theology as well as on his particular methodology, that is, the keys and dynamics operative in his thought. Specifically the keys and dynamics will deal with the significance of Panikkar's cosmotheandric vision, the importance he gives to individual and collective religious experiences and intrareligious dialogue, his statement that the trinitarian experience is an all-embracing universal experience of the Divine and finally the importance of Christianity as a truly universal religion. The final section of this chapter will indicate the difficulties of Panikkar's terminology, including what he borrows from various theological schools as well as his original terminology.

Chapter II will examine the earlier trinitarian thought of Panikkar. It will be divided into four sections. Section A will describe Panikkar's earliest thought on the Trinity as he connects it with the Advaita Vedanta system in Hinduism. The text examined is the first edition of *The Unknown Christ of Hinduism* (1964).[2] Section B will study Panikkar's work entitled *The Trinity and the Religious Experience of Man* (1973).[3] *Icon-Person-Mystery* (Madras: The Christian Literature Society, 1970). Section C will examine the other works of the earlier Panikkar. A brief summary of Panikkar's early thought will be given in the final section.

Chapter III will examine the later trinitarian thought of Panikkar. Section A will point out the significant changes made to the second edition of *The Unknown Christ of Hinduism* (1981) as it relates to his concept of Trinity. Sections B, C, D and E will explore other material indicating further development and shifts in Panikkar's position on the Trinity. These latter sections will address one of his latest trinitarian articles (1987),[4] his prestigious Gifford Lectures (1989),[5] his University of Tulsa Warren Lecture (1991)[6] as well as his Cardinal Bellarmine Lecture (1991).[7] The chapter will conclude with a brief summary of Panikkar's later thought.

Chapter IV will present a résumé and an evaluation of Panikkar's thought on the Trinity. Section A will provide a summary of the development of the trinitarian thought of the earlier and the later Panikkar. The first part will point out areas of both continuity and shifts between the 1964 and 1981 edition of *The Unknown Christ of Hinduism*. The second part of the section will indicate continuity and shifts drawing from all his works related to the Trinity. Section B will offer a critique of his thought from several prospectives. Panikkar's methodology in light of the formative factors of theology will be evaluated. Varied assessments of his thought by other authors will then be presented. A general evaluation of the continuity and shifts of Panikkar's thought will follow with a concluding assessment of his overall proposal.

In Chapter V the problems deriving from Panikkar's concept of the Trinity will be examined. Are history and Christianity taken seriously? How unique is the historical Jesus? Is Panikkar advocating a new ecumenical religion? Is he undermining the traditional understanding of missiology?

Finally there will be a short conclusion, followed by a bibliography.

Notes

1   Panikkar has used three different first names. He now uses the Spanish version Raimon. Previously he used Raymond and Raimundo.
2   There are two editions of this text. Raimundo Panikkar, *The Unknown Christ of Hinduism* (London: Darton, Longman and Todd, 1964); *The Unknown Christ of Hinduism: Towards an Ecumenical Christophany* (Maryknoll: Orbis Books, 1981).
3   Raimundo Panikkar, *The Trinity and the Religious Experience of Man. Icon-Person-Mystery* (London: Darton, Longman and Todd, 1973). The Indian edition is entitled *The Trinity and World Religions.*
4   Raimundo Panikkar, "The Jordan, the Tiber, and the Ganges: Three Kairological Moments of Christic Self-Consciousness," in *The Myth of Christian Uniqueness: Toward a Pluralistic Theology of Religion*, ed. John Hick and Paul Knitter (Maryknoll: Orbis Books, 1987), 89-116.
5   Raimon Panikkar, *Gifford Lectures: Trinity and Atheism: The Housing of the Divine in the Contemporary World* (A series of ten lectures given at University of Edinburgh, April 25-May 12, 1989, to be published by Orbis Books under the title of *The Rhythm of Being*). A brief summary of Lecture Six, entitled "The Radical Trinity", is given in Chapter III.
6   Raimon Panikkar, *On Catholic Identity. University of Tulsa, Warren Lecture: Catholic Studies, No. 17* (Tulsa: University of Tulsa, 1991).
7   Raimon Panikkar, *Cardinal Bellarmine Lecture*: "A Christophany for Our Times," *Theology Digest* 39 (1992): 3-21.

Chapter I

Panikkar: Context, Methodology, Terminology

A. Context

1. Biography

The range of Panikkar's background is enormously wide and complex. This circumstance accounts for some of the difficulty in understanding his writings. He was born in Barcelona, Spain, November 3, 1918, of an Indian Hindu father and a Spanish Catholic mother. He grew up in a Hindu-Catholic environment, learning the Hindu Scriptures alongside the Christian Bible. In 1946 at the age of 28, he received a doctorate in philosophy from the University of Madrid. The same year he was ordained a Roman Catholic Priest. In 1955 his longing to discover and experience the Ultimate beyond the boundaries of Catholicism took him to India to study Indian philosophy and religion. His interest in the sciences, moreover, was also strong. In 1958 he received a doctorate in chemistry from the University of Madrid. His collective findings involved him in further study of theology. In 1961 he received a doctorate in theology from the Lateran University in Rome. During the same year he was instrumental as a "founding father" of the Castelli Conferences on Hermeneutics at the University of Rome. While maintaining close contact with the East, Panikkar moved to the United States as a professor at Harvard University (1967) and at the University of California, Santa Barbara (1971). His interest in experiencing and expressing the Ultimate took on new dimensions and deeper forms as he penetrated the Hindu and Buddhist Scriptures and continued to dialogue and pray with adherents of other religious disciplines, especially Hindus and Buddhists.

Panikkar has made contributions in the area of history of religions, comparative religion, hermeneutics, theology, interreligious dialogue, philosophy, education, indology and the sciences, in particular, chemistry. He has been a member of many learned societies and associations and a director on the boards of several journals.

Panikkar has made his mark not only in the academic world but also in the area of spirituality. Ignatius Hirudayam comments, "In India a series of anthologies have been published to be added to the official prayer of the church. Raimundo Panikkar's *Vedic Experience. Mantramanjari* is an eminent work of this kind."[1]

Standing on the boundary between Hinduism and Christianity, he has moved further into the cultural and religious experience of both East and West. His contact with Buddhism has plunged him into a new dimension of religious experience and provided him with new categories in which to speak of the Ultimate.

One of his earliest major works on Trinity, *The Trinity and the Religious Experience of Man*, was written around 1963 and published in 1973. "This study was written ten years ago in Uttarkashi in the heart of the Himalayas in a small hut on the shore of the Ganges."[2] This was preceded by his famous work, *The Unknown Christ of Hinduism*, written in 1957 and published in 1964.

Most of Panikkar's later works (1976 - 93), which include approximately thirty books and over three hundred articles, deal with history of religions, theology and hermeneutics. Many of these works reflect Panikkar's trinitarian thought.

He has lately chosen to live quietly in Tavertet, Spain. He continues close contact with the East and is a citizen of India. Occasionally he accepts invitations to lecture outside of Spain. In 1989 he gave the celebrated Gifford Lectures at the University of Edinburgh. In 1991 he delivered the University of Tulsa Warren Lecture. That year he also presented the Cardinal Bellarmine Lecture.

2. Theological Transition & Turmoil

Panikkar's theology has been hammered out in a period of widespread theological transition and crisis, with theology in general facing the challenge of radical renewal. Panikkar developed his trinitarian thought as well as his Christology at a time when he saw the problem of Christ and the world religions to be significant and urgent.

This prevalent theological crisis[3] is intensified by the communications explosion and by a new wave of encounters between adherents of the various world religions and cultures. Contact between Christianity and other world religions is taking place in a way never before possible, with Christianity being challenged to rethink its theological positions, even in such central areas as Trinity and Christology.

The God question affecting the relationship between Christianity and other religions has erupted into a major theological explosion with a proliferation of publications such as Paul F. Knitter's *No Other Name?*[4] and others[5]. The shift towards theocentrism, espoused by theologians such as John Hick, has left theology in the twentieth century with an urgent need for synthesis, leading either to deeper adherence to the basic tenets of traditional Christianity or to a flat rejection of the uniqueness of Jesus of Nazareth.

There are more traditional voices, like that of Cardinal Ratzinger, claiming that the value of non-Christian religions is being overemphasized by those who assert that other religions are not *"extraordinary* paths of salvation but precisely *ordinary* ones."[6] Ratzinger insists that in confronting the world religions Christ still needs to be proclaimed. The Cardinal emphasizes that "there is only one mediator between God and men, the man Christ Jesus, who gave himself as a ransom for all." (1 Tim. 2:7)[7] But on the other hand, there are writers who, in their assessment of official Catholic statements on other religions complain that, although the Church has made giant strides in its approach to religions such as Hinduism and Buddhism, relationships with them are still unsatisfactory because of ignorance of their sprirtual depths on the part of Christians.

3. Lack of an Adequate Theology of Religion

Panikkar has developed his framework of Trinity at a time when Catholic thought suffered from an inadequate theology of religion. He explains "we do not possess so far a theology of religion worth the name for the geographical and historical coordinates of our times."[8] This same criticism is made by a number of theologians[9] who have experienced other living faiths in the arena of missionary action or inter-faith dialogue. They contend that in confrontation with other religions, theology of religion for most Christian authors is regarded as a particular theology of a particular religion that is then generalized or expressed in universal terms.

Even Vatican II's Declaration on the Relationship of the Church to Non-Christian Religions, *Nostra Aetate*, has been judged less than satisfactory for this same reason: "the heart of the problem in the document is the Church's theology of religions."[10] Another author remarks:

> These men of whom the Declaration speaks all happen to believe sincerely that their own religions are the truth. Yet they are addressed by the Council Fathers as if they were misguided children who surprisingly manifest on occasion a certain amount of good sense. The overall impression created by the Declaration is certainly, though not intentionally, one of benign condescension.[11]

The new pluralistic consciousness is giving rise to a theology of religion that is no longer based on a superficial evaluation of the world religions, especially Hinduism and Buddhism. Nevertheless, one aspect of these religions continues to be undermined, ignored or superficially treated: the internal experiential dimension. When dealing specifically with the doctrine of Trinity, the situation is even more complex. This is precisely because even Christians usually do not consciously advert to Trinity, despite their confessional belief in the doctrine. Practically, they are "mere 'monotheists.'"[12] The Trinity is more an object of formal belief than a datum of everyday experience. Because the core of Hinduism, especially the Advaita[13] Vedanta school, and most schools of Buddhism[14] are essentially grounded on the experiential awareness of the Ultimate, the internal dimension of these religions is vitally important in any discussion of the doctrine of Trinity in relation to these world religions.

Panikkar is convinced that the internal experiential dimension of a particular religion cannot be bypassed or ignored, or vaguely and superficially dealt with in an authentic theology of religion. The living faiths "cannot adequately be expressed in any written form whatsoever."[15] Mere phenomenology of religion cannot suffice as theology of religion. An authentic theology of religion valid for the study of world religions requires to some degree an ability to experience another religion or at least acknowledge that it is "possible to have the internal and authentic experience of more than one religion."[16]

Panikkar emphasizes that, "only if we delve deeply into the study *and* practice of religions can we understand one another, and only then is a mutual fecundation possible."[17] It is necessary for the development of an authentic theology of religion, not only to take religions such as Hinduism seriously, but also to experience them from within and even to believe in those religions.[18] Panikkar holds, together with other theologians, especially in the area of missiology, that it is crucial to have an authentic theology of religion before one is able to comprehend the spiritual wealth that is present in the different world religions.

In summary, Panikkar's development of a trinitarian theology has taken place in a period marked by theological turmoil, theological shifts and pluralistic consciousness without the aid of an adequate theology of religion.

B. Methodology

Panikkar's theological method will be considered in two sections, general and particular. The general section will describe his methodology in the light of traditional Catholic categories. The second section will elucidate the particular insights and emphases employed by Panikkar.

1. General Methodology: Panikkar's Methodology In the Light of Formative Factors of Theology

The Scottish Anglican theologian, John Macquarrie, speaks of "formative factors of theology,"[19] roughly equivalent to the sources or "loci theologici" of classical Roman Catholic theology. The factors are: experience, revelation, scripture, tradition, culture and reason. To his list will be added two other factors or sources that are indispensable from a Roman Catholic viewpoint: magisterium and liturgy.

Macquarrie insists that at the beginning of his work the theologian must explicitate the major factors involved and must resolve to accord each one its due weight. Otherwise, one-sided simplifications (such as biblicism and traditionalism), if not even more serious distortions, result. The ideal is to recognize the real tensions among the formative factors and to allow for a dialectical interplay. Macquarrie warns that only in this way can a theology meet "the demands that it should be loyal to the faith which it seeks to express, yet pertinent to the cultural environment which it seeks to address."[20]

a) Experience

Experience appears first on Macquarrie's list because, as he explains, "some experience of the life of faith precedes theology and may indeed be said to motivate it."[21] Experience is paramount in the trinitarian thought of Panikkar. In his *The Unknown Christ of Hinduism* (1964, 1981) he employs a religious system that pivots on the experience of the Advaitin. Panikkar formulates his concept of the Trinity with the experience of Isvara as the Christ.

In his major trinitarian work, *Trinity and the Religious Experience of Man* (1973), he draws on the experience of adherents to Buddhism, Hinduism and Christianity in arriving at his universal framework of Trinity, as follows. As for Buddhism, he uses the category of Nirvana to best express the apophatic approach to the Father, the First Person of the Trinity. This category is purely experiential. Not much can be said about it, except that it is non-expressible, pure experience. As for Hinduism, the Advaita system, which Panikkar utilizes to bring out the Spirit dimension of the Trinity, is also highly experiential. Also Bhakti tradition (loving devotion) operates from the perspective of experience, although not with the totality found in the experience of Advaita. As for Christianity, Panikkar affirms the Christian experience of loving devotion as the centre of Christian spirituality.

Regarding Panikkar's own personal experience, he declares, " . . . I start from the existential situation in which I happen to be. I affirm that I am starting from my personal situation and faith . . . "[23] When Panikkar mentions "my personal situation and faith," he is referring to his personal allegiance, not only to Christianity, but also to Hinduism, and, in his later years, also to Buddhism. Throughout he insists that "one's own experience is indispensable."[24]

b) Revelation

Macquarrie calls revelation "the primary source of theology, and also a basic category in theological thinking."[25] Panikkar draws on several sources of revelation, since in the development of his trinitarian thought he is functioning within several religious systems. He appeals, primarily, to Christian revelation in the early stages of his thought. He would agree with Macquarrie that "In the Christian religion, a person, Jesus Christ, is the bearer of revelation."[26] Panikkar's later thought, however, presupposes revelation as coming almost equally through other religions and even beyond the boundaries of religion in the depths of the human person.

c) *Scripture*

Next Macquarrie introduces scripture, which he presents, together with tradition as mediating the primordial revelation. Panikkar uses the Christian Scriptures, both Old and New Testaments, extensively. He is constantly referring especially to the Gospels as he develops his trinitarian thought.

Nevertheless, since the later Panikkar does not recognize Jesus Christ as the primary bearer of revelation for all of humanity, the way he employs the Christian Scripture is affected. In addition, he draws readily on the Scriptures of other traditions, especially Hinduism. The use of these non-Christian Scriptures has led to a nuancing of his interpretation of the Christian Scriptures.

In this connection it is noteworthy to record how Macquarrie warns against extravagant attempts on the part of some contemporary Christian biblical theologians "to imply that only biblical categories are proper to theological thinking." Macquarrie responds:

> Actually, the Christian faith has extended itself both in time and space because of its ability to interpret itself in ever new categories. We are all agreed that theology must keep in close touch with its biblical sources, but to try to exclude non-biblical sources is absurd.[27]

This is precisely what Panikkar sets out to do: he adheres closely to Christian biblical sources without excluding non-biblical sources.

d) *Tradition*

Among the formative factors of theology Macquarrie next includes tradition. He assigns it an indispensable role in Christian theology, especially for Catholics. Macquarrie cautions against two extremes with regard to tradition. The one extreme would be minimalistic, that is, to "break with tradition either for the sake of being modern or for the sake (as they imagine) of going right back to the New Testament, as if all the intervening development could be left out."[28] The other extreme would be maximalistic: a notion of tradition that is excessive, rigid, uncritical and mechanical, "so that all growth and healthy development are inhibited."[29] Macquarrie reminds us that ancient interpretations of the faith, such as the doctrine of the Trinity, cannot be discarded without destroying the community, but that there needs to be continual reinterpretation of ancient formulas into current categories of thought.

Panikkar, especially in his earlier stages, links his trinitarian thought with certain strains in the Christian past. For example, Cousins views Panikkar's early trinitarian theology as having an affinity with the trinitarian thought of the Greek Fathers and the early Franciscan school.[30]

Panikkar's use of non-Christian traditions is very prominent. He appeals to Hindu traditions in order to formulate new categories. For example, he examines the development of Isvara[31] within Hinduism and introduces this category into his trinitarian framework. Another example of Panikkar's attention to Hindu tradition is his use of the insights of the Advaita Vedanta school, which is a major development from the original Vedas of Hinduism.

In summary, Panikkar is working out of three major traditions: Christianity, Hinduism and Buddhism. He attempts to merge some of the insights of all three traditions in his trinitarian theology. Certainly he succeeds in avoiding the maximalistic extreme of viewing tradition in a rigid, uncritical way without any reinterpretation. The question remains whether he sufficiently avoids the minimalistic extreme of breaking with the tradition for the sake of being relevant.

e) Culture

The next formative factor of theology discussed by Macquarrie is culture. Macquarrie reminds us first of all that all religious language, including that of the Bible, is culturally conditioned and therefore in constant need of reinterpretation. Once more, Macquarrie points out the necessity of maintaining a fine balance between two poles: on the one hand, there is the demand for relevance and intelligibility; on the other hand, there is the need for truth and continuity. Failure to maintain this balance leads to a one-sided embracing of one or the other of the two poles. Thus, one extreme would accommodate and subordinate the revelation to the culture; the other extreme would insulate the revelation against all contact with the changing forms of other cultures.

Macquarrie writes, " . . . there is a variable element in theology as it addresses itself to its own day . . . in terms of the prevailing cultural forms. It may even be the case that in the use of ideas taken over from the contemporary culture, deeper insights are gained into the revelation that has been passed on."[32]

How does Panikkar make use of the formative factor of culture in his trinitarian methodology? Obviously, this factor looms very large for Panikkar. First of all, he attempts in a general way to do exactly what is suggested by Macquarrie: both to retain the core of the truth of the

Trinity and also to reinterpret this truth in an even more relevant and intelligible manner. Also, in particular, Panikkar follows what Macquarrie recommends by seeking to express the Trinity in ways even more relevant for an Eastern audience. For example, he speaks of homeomorphic equivalents and Christophany.

In addition, Panikkar's concern for the demands of culture goes even beyond what Macquarrie suggests insofar as Panikkar becomes transcultural. Panikkar has written much on various cultures, especially Hinduism and Buddhism, and their interaction with Christianity. Likewise, he applies these insights to his trinitarian theology. He is able to move from a category within one culture to a category within another culture as he refines his trinitarian thought.

Panikkar's trinitarian framework exemplifies what John Dunne refers to as "passing over" and "coming back."[34] The cultural "crossing over" in which Panikkar has been engaged most of his life has resulted in a development of his thought that is far from linear. "I have not adopted the view of a linear development of human thought, as if we could now encompass in one single system the multicolored human wisdom throughout the ages."[35]

Cousins describes Panikkar as one who has " 'stood on the boundary,' not primarily between religion and secular culture, but between diverse cultures themselves in their religious depth."[36] It is from standing on this "boundary" that his concept of Trinity takes on a new dimension.

f) Reason

The last formative factor considered by Macquarrie is reason. After stating that almost all theologians would allow some place to reason, Macquarrie affirms that currently the "overprizing of reason seems to be less of a danger than that reason's place should be underestimated."[37] The prevailing climate is anti-speculative.

Macquarrie divides reason into speculative and critical. Speculative reason seeks to construct "a metaphysic or theory of reality."[38] Macquarrie holds that a theology for today should "avoid any heavy dependency on speculative reason."[39] However, he maintains that there seems to be a function of reason somewhat similar to its speculative exercise, yet in some ways distinct from it. He calls it the architectonic function of reason: "a constructive use of reason in which we build up rational wholes, theories or interlocking systems of ideas, but do so not by deductive argument but rather by imaginative leaps . . . "[40] Karl Barth is given as the obvious example.

Returning to his broad distinction between speculative and critical reason, Macquarrie turns to the latter and subdivides it into the elucidatory and the corrective exercises of reason. He explains that "elucidatory reason" would be acknowledged even by theologians who have a rather negative attitude to reason. Elucidatory reason "sifts, analyzes, expands, expounds, and, generally speaking, brings into the light the content of the revelation."[41]

Corrective reason gives the rational element in theology a much more prominent role without, however, achieving the level of speculative reason. Corrective reason examines the revelation: questions its claims, criticizes it, purifies it from defects. If not a rational religion, at least the ideal of a reasonable religion should be upheld.[42] Macquarrie strongly endorses reason as a formative factor in theology and includes not only elucidatory reason, but also corrective and architectonic reason.

The theological formative factor of reason plays a crucial role in Panikkar's methodology which will now be examined in light of the three types of reason just presented from Macquarrie. These will be considered in ascending order of the importance accorded to reason in theological method.

"Elucidatory reason" naturally has a place in Panikkar's methodology. He is constantly anaylzing, expanding and bringing into the light the content of trinitarian revelation. For example, in his effort to make sense of the Christian Trinity within the Advaita school of Hinduism, Panikkar elucidates the Advaita experience in terms of non-duality by connecting the Advaita experience with the experience of the Spirit. In trying to place Isvara as the Christ in Hinduism, Panikkar traces the development of the concept of Isvara in Indian literature and argues for a place for Isvara that is both authentic to the Hindu world and elucidatory of the trinitarian theology that he is envisioning.

"Corrective reason" also is an important aspect of Panikkar's methodology. He examines trinitarian doctrine by questioning its claims, critiquing it and seeking to purge it from historical defects. The classic example of this is the way Panikkar tries to expand and deepen the Christian concept of the Trinity to include all religious experiences, especially the Nirvana experience in Buddhism. His expansion of the concept of the Trinity in his later thought stretches even beyond the confines of religious structures into the secular world.

The third and strongest use of reason of the three types presented by Macquarrie is "architectonic reason." This too is embraced vigorously by Panikkar. In keeping with "architectonic reason" he constructively elaborates his system of trinitarian thought, not so much by deductive argument as by imaginative leaps.

In summary, it is clear that in his earlier thought the foundation out of which Panikkar builds his concept of the Trinity remains mainly within the context of the world religions. Drawing from anthropology, science, mathematics, philosophy, religion, present day consciousness of the human person and the contemporary global situation, Panikkar rebuilds his structure of the Trinity through careful use of reason. In his later trinitarian thought Panikkar claims that, although reason may not be the highest tribunal, it is the first jurisdiction and has the right to send to a possible higher instance those cases that reason itself judges to supersede the competence of reason.[43] Panikkar insists that in order to experience the Trinity, contact with reality is required through the senses, the intellect and the mystical,[44] even beyond any religious structures. Paradoxically, through reason, Panikkar somewhat downplays reason and seeks to show its interconnectedness with other "organs" or faculties as he moves dramatically to new horizons in his treatment of the Trinty.[45]

g) *Magisterium*

Even though Macquarrie lists only the aforementioned six formative factors of theology, there are two additional factors or sources of theology that must be taken into account by any Roman Catholic theologian: magisterium and liturgy. These two will now be treated and the question raised whether and to what extent Panikkar employs them in his theologizing.

First, the magisterium will be addressed. For Roman Catholics the hierarchical or ecclesiastical magisterium is an indispensable factor or source of theology.[46] The magisterium is understood as the authority to proclaim and teach officially in the Church. This authority belongs exclusively a) to the entire college of bishops (as successors to the apostolic college) and to the individual bishops united with the Bishop of Rome and b) to the Pope. Both the bishops and the Pope exercise a day-to-day or ordinary magisterium in addition to a solemn or extraordinary one.[47]

Much has been written lately about the relationship between the theologian and the magisterium.[48] The most helpful treatment of this question has been offered in 1975 by the International Theological Commission's Document, "Theses on the Relationship between the Ecclesiastical Magisterium and Theology."[49] These theses seem to "reflect a fairly broad consensus in the Catholic theological Community."[50]

The background of the current literature in this general area is the inevitable tension between theologians and the magisterium, especially of late in the area of difficulties with or dissent from non-infallible but authoritative teaching. Both sides in the dialogue agree in general that, although theologians have a responsibility to take seriously authoritative pronouncements, assent to such teaching must be "nuanced according to the intent, contents, arguments, and promulgating authority of the position."[51]

Of the International Theological Commission's twelve "Theses" only those that most bear on this dissertation will now be addressed and each time the question will be raised: To what extent does Panikkar employ the hierarchical magisterium as a factor or *locus* of theology.

i. It is the task of theologians "to safeguard the deposit of revelation, to seek ever deeper insight into it, to explain, teach and defend it." (from Thesis 2)

In the development of his trinitarian thought, Panikkar does seek to deepen and expand the Christian concept of the Trinity and also to present it in such a way that it may be accessible to other religious traditions. Panikkar tries at great length to teach and to explain. As a theologian he sees his mission as making the Trinity credible for all peoples. Panikkar sees his task as that of a missionary. However, in the process, the question is raised whether he adequately safeguards the deposit of revelation or in any way defends it.

ii. Theologians are "bound by the documents of Tradition" and cannot "neglect such records of the faith." (from Thesis 3)

Panikkar spends very little time rooting his thought in the "documents of Tradition." For example, in his major trinitarian writings there are few references to the early Church's general councils dealing with the Trinity: the Council of Nicaea (325) on the identity of the Logos and the Council of Constantinople I (381) on the divinity of the Holy Spirit. However, he does refer once to the Council of Chalcedon's famous four qualifications on the two natures in Christ.[52] *A fortiori* Panikkar takes no pains to address documents of the ordinary magisterium.

iii. There should be "co-responsible cooperation and collegial association" between theologians and the magisterium. (from Thesis 4)

In the development of Panikkar's trinitarian thought, there is no explicit evidence of any particular cooperation and collegial association between Panikkar and the magisterium. However, in his earlier writings, his general tone and orientation is more in keeping with official Catholic teaching.

iv. "The theologians' function can be described as one of mediating - in both directions -between the magisterium and the people of God." (from Thesis 5)

This two-fold mediation takes place: "from the faith, culture and questionings of the people toward the magisterium; and from the pronouncements of the magisterium back to the people."[53]

As for the mediating movement from the people of God toward the magisterium, Panikkar can be said to qualify very positively, albeit in a very implicit way. That is, although he does not specifically request or challenge the magisterium to respect the faith, culture and questionings of the people in the area of Trinity, nevertheless the entire thrust of his writing on Trinity is a plea that the insights and concerns of Hindu traditions be respected and assimilated in ongoing formulation of trinitarian doctrine.

As for the mediating movement from the magisterium toward the people of God, this is not Panikkar's concern. Although he respects past formulations of magisterial statements on Trinity, he is very quick to point out their limitations and even to work toward re-formulation.

h) Liturgy

The final formative factor or *locus* of theology to be considered is liturgy.[54] Following the lead of Vatican Council II's 1963 Constitution on the Sacred Liturgy, *Sacrosanctum Concilium*, Catholic theology in the West has become more aware of the liturgy as a true source of theology.[55]

Eastern theology has always recognized that all prayer, and, in an eminent way, liturgical prayer, play an indispensable role in the interpretation of Christian faith.[56] Even in the Western Church there has been throughout its history interaction between worship and belief. Avery Dulles explains that, "sometimes the approved modes of worship give rise to doctrines, and sometimes worship is deliberately modified to reflect and inculcate the church's teaching."[57]

This dynamic is expressed in the axiom, "lex orandi est lex credendi."[58] Unfortunately, in their theologizing Western writers have sometimes given only lip service to this axiom. However, of late, and especially since the Second Vatican Council, Catholic theologians in the West have become increasingly aware of the liturgy as an effective source of theology.[59]   Vagaggini was one of the pioneers before the Council.[60] Congar is exemplary as a contemporary Western theologian who draws effectively on liturgy as a source of his theologizing.[61]

Aidan Nichols insightfully points to the liturgy and Christian art as mediations of tradition in words that apply equally well to describing liturgy as a formative factor or *locus* of theology:

> . . . the liturgy is the continuation of the atoning work of Jesus Christ and, as such, is the Church's primary expression from within of the covenant relationship binding her life to God's. It is, therefore, rich in implicit theology. The texts of a wide variety of liturgies are all grist for the theologian's mill. However, the greater the agreement of these liturgies on a particular point, the stronger their evidential value for theology. If we think of the Christian liturgy as a sign system pointing to the truth of Tradition, it is where the signals flash most brightly that we can best follow them.[62]

Panikkar addresses the question of worship in his *Worship and Secular Man*.[63]   It deals with the general interraction between secularity and worship with an application to Hinduism. In this work Panikkar does not deal with trinitarian themes.

2. Particular Methodology: Keys and Dynamics of Panikkar's Trinitarian Thought

There are several keys and dynamics in Panikkar's thought that lie at the heart of Panikkar's attempt to penetrate the concept of the Trinity in such a manner as to join the in-depth religious experiences of the world religions with human experience in general. The keys to his thought include his cosmotheandric vision; individual and collective religious experience of the world religions; intrareligious dialogue; the concept of the Trinity as an all-embracing universal experience of the Divine; and his recognition and interpretation of Christianity as a truly universal religion having meaning for all peoples.

These elements, combined and reinforced by the dynamics of Panikkar's unique insights, result in an original interpretation of the Trinity and new possibilities presented by this interpretation. The dynamics of this conception become mobilized by his vision that at the heart of the experience of the world religions and of the Divine in the secular world, both individually and collectively, lies the experience of the Trinity.

a) *Theandric (Cosmotheandric) Vision*[64]

The main key to Panikkar's thought is his foundational concept of theandrism. He defines theandrism as "the classical and traditional term for that intimate and complete unity which is realized paradigmatically in Christ between the divine and the human and which is the goal towards which everything here below tends - in Christ and the Spirit."[65]

Theandrism brings out the two elements that Panikkar uses in addressing the various spiritualities found among the world religions: the "human element which serves as the point of departure and the transhuman factor."[66] For him the religious consciousness of everyone evolves towards the Divine that permeates and envelops humanity transforming all from within. The human person is intimately connected with the Divine. Humans are not separate beings requiring an external supernatural force to elevate them through a dramatic external intervention. They are not totally separate from a God whom they serve and worship. Their nature is such that they have a spark of the Divine within. Their natural tendency is a yearning to be encompassed by the Divine bringing them to their fullest potential. As Christ was at the same time divine and human, so must all human persons strive towards their highest potential, which means total unity with God. All are destined to be sons and daughters of God, to be one with Christ, who was both divine and human in total unity. Human persons are not separate entities looking out upon their God with their God looking down upon them. Their God is stamped upon their innermost being in order for them to become who they were destined to be in unity with the Divine, to be truly genuine sons and daughters of the Most High, to be brothers and sisters of Christ in the Holy Spirit.

Theandrism for Panikkar incorporates the full language and teachings of Christianity; morever, its foundational use in his thought serves as special groundwork for what will follow.[67] Theandrism will provide fertile soil for the concept of Atman equals Brahman: the innermost Self is equal to God;[68] there is non-duality in the relationship between the human being and God, the self (with a common 's') must give way to the Self within (with a capital 'S').

The dynamics of Panikkar's probing tools provide further links between concepts in Christianity and concepts in the world religions, in particular the Advaita Vedanta system in Hinduism and some key concepts in Buddhism. "God and man are, so to speak, in close constitutive collaboration for the building-up of reality, the unfolding of history and the continuation of creation."[69] The entire human race, God and all of reality are evolving together to make all things new. There is a Divine Oneness that pervades all of reality: the cosmos and all of humanity. The journey unveils the past, present and future in the Divine and new creation.

The Mandukya Upanishad begins as follows:

> HARIH AUM! AUM, the word, is all this. All that is past, present and future is, indeed, Aum. And whatever else there is, beyond the threefold division of time - that also is truly Aum. All this is, indeed, Brahman. This Atman is Brahman.[70]

In his introduction to the Mandukya Upanishad, Swami Nikhilananda writes, "Unlike the other Upanisads, the Mandukya Upanisad . . . plunges at once into a discussion of Brahman and Atman, the innermost essence of the universe and of man, and proclaims that they are non-different."[71]

Panikkar also establishes a radical identification: "There is a movement, a dynamism, a growth in what Christians call the mystical Body of Christ and Buddhists call *dharmakaya*."[72] He makes continous references to such concepts as "the Mystical Body of Christ," firmly rooted in the Christ Event. He then links these concepts with categories from other religious traditions, such as the *dharmakaya* or another one of the bodies of the Buddha. The *dharmakaya* also finds itself in the realm of mystery; however, the tradition and the experiential context out of which the concept of the *dharmakaya* develops is radically different from that of the Christ Event. Panikkar's later thought moved away from the person of the Buddha and the three bodies of the Buddha as equivalent to Krishna or Jesus to a more developed concept that he termed the "homeomorphic equivalents." "The so-called non-christians find, discover, believe in the *homeomorphic equivalents* of what Christians call the christ in and through other symbols."[73] Although Panikkar's concepts may stem from very diverse religious traditions, he finds unity in his comparison of individual and collective religious experiences.

b) Individual and Collective Religious Experiences

The set of spiritualities continuously functioning in Panikkar's thought is based on individual and collective religious experiences within the great world religions, although it is evident from his writing that he has an affinity for Christianity, Hinduism and Buddhism as the umbrella religions with which he is experientially involved.

The three major spiritualities proposed by Panikkar in his initial treatment of Trinity are based: first, on the experience of Nirvana in

Buddhism; secondly, on the experience of loving devotion in Christianity and the Bhakti tradition in Hinduism; and thirdly, on the experience of non-duality in the Advaita Vedanta tradition in Hinduism.

Among these religions Panikkar finds structures which will give his thought a unique flexibility and will inform his reformulation of the concept of the Trinity, although he eventually moves "beyond" these religions in his mature thought. As seen earlier, experience plays an important role in Panikkar's general methodology and his selection of terms. It is by searching on the experiential level for the foundation of the various spiritualities that Panikkar finds the impetus to forge ahead with bold categories to a reformulation of the Trinity. The traditions with which he works are highly experiential. They are experiential on the part of the individual seeking to attain non-duality in the Advaita Vedanta tradition or seeking Nirvana or enlightenment in Buddhism. They are also experiential collectively as in scriptural directives or in the use of communal concepts such as the Trikaya (Three Bodies of the Buddha) developed by the later Mahayana schools of Buddhism.

c) *Intrareligious Dialogue*

Panikkar posits intrareligious dialogue as extremely significant in the interpretive process, as he analyzes his trinitarian concept in conjunction with the world religions. Podgorski describes Panikkar's understanding of mutual in-depth religious encounters as follows, "When 'dialogical dialogue' occurs, *homo viator* may be aided by the Buddhist to enhance her wonder at the 'Mystery Immanent,' from the Christian she may learn to deepen her awe before the 'mystery Transcendent...'"[74] Podgorski also emphasizes that in Panikkar's book *The Intrareligious Dialogue* he proposes intrareligious dialogue "as the paradigm and interpretive hermeneutic for the authentic religious experience of our era."[75]

It is in the ultimate experience of loving God that two individuals from different traditions find themselves experiencing the Trinity. Panikkar affirms, "God is the unique locus where my selfhood and my neighbour's coincide, consequently the one place that enables me to love him as he loves his own self without any attempt at molding him."[76]

When the two opposing views meet deep within an individual, then "dialogue prompts genuine religious pondering, and even a religious crisis, at the bottom of a Man's heart".[77] It is at this point that interpersonal dialogue becomes transformed into interpersonal soliloquy. Genuine dialogue is not "bare methodology"; it is an "essential part of the religious act *par excellence.*"[78] Panikkar declares that our "neighbour's faith is part of our own religious development."[79] It is critical that we "attain the religious *experience* of our cocitizens . . ."[80] Panikkar maintains that in intrareligious dialogue "True intimacy does not stiffen or deaden us, because within that Self (God is not the Other, he is the One) dwell life, dialogue and love. This is in fact the trinitarian mystery. . ."[81]

d) Trinity as Universal Experience of the Divine

The Trinity as seen by Panikkar is not a lifeless abstract concept with little bearing on reality. For him the Trinity is firmly rooted in universal experience: not one or two sets of experiences but numerous sets of religious experiences which in his earlier works can be broadly categorized under the three major spiritualities. His later works reflect these sets of experiences under categories that move beyond religious systems into the secular world. In one of his earliest works on the Trinity (1973), Panikkar compares the term "trinitarian" with the term "theandric" to express the synthesis of catholic universal religious experience. He explains:

> I prefer the term *theandric* to the term *trinitarian* to describe this synthesis and the whole catholic (*kath'holon*) spirituality in which it culminates. The first reason for this is that current theology has too often relegated the trinitarian mystery to the exclusive sphere of the Divinity, 'theology' in the Greek use of the word i.e. the study of God-in-himself totally or almost independent of the 'economy' or study of God in his 'temporal manifestation', i.e. creation and incarnation. A *trinitarian* spirituality in the strict sense of the word might run the risk of not conceding, or at least of not sufficiently manifesting, the necessity of the dimension of incarnation, of humanity, without which every synthesis remains inevitably impoverished. Another reason for avoiding this term is that, since the Trinity is the central dogma of Christianity, it is in christian faith where this essential mystery of the divine life, even of the whole of reality is thematically developed, whatever the 'adumbrations' of it that may be discerned elsewhere, while I would prefer a term without such direct christian connotations.[82]

This work, although published in 1973, had been written ten years earlier. There are already overtones that Panikkar is moving away from traditional Christian trinitarian thought to a more universal perspective in his attempt to come to grips with a concept of the Trinity that he understands to be in need of broadening.

It is important to note that Panikkar's use of the term "incarnation" in the above quotation is pregnant with universal connotations that take into account the multiple experiences of the Divine. The term "incarnation" includes mediators of Eastern thought on numerous levels. In addition, Panikkar's belief that the trinitarian experience is embraced by people of all cultures and religions is enriched by the new dimensions he brings to it. However, the complexity also increases.

e) *Christianity As A Universal Religion*

Christianity is traditionally viewed by Christians as a religion containing the fullness of revelation. However, for Panikkar, when Christianity is viewed from the centre as having the fullness of revelation with the other religions remaining outside, showing only "rays of light" or reflections of that one truth, then Christianity's universality is compromised. Christianity is one of many religions, each of which brings its own gifts and insights and reveals God's communication with his people and the human family's communication with their God over the centuries. A general overview of Panikkar's works indicates that he argues for a plurality of religions, each equally authentic in itself.

The underlying factor in Panikkar's thought allowing him the flexibility to reformulate the trinitarian concept and develop an original Christology is his belief that Christianity (based on his unique notion of Christ) is a truly universal religion. He also holds that there is only one universal Church. It must be remembered, though, that for Panikkar the "one universal Church" transcends Christianity. The Logos (whom Panikkar equates with "Christ"), incarnate and risen, is visibly and also invisibly present in all religions. The Logos is experienced in the many religious figures present in the world religions. Wherever the Trinity is present, according to Panikkar's trinitarian concept, there the Church is also present.

His overarching view of the Trinity is the universal paradigm that Panikkar uses to encompass and envelop the world religions and at the same time allow them to retain their own uniqueness and individuality in the process. He uses the concretized expression of the various religious experiences as seen within the different spiritualities[83] to show that the Trinity is to be experienced in a multifaceted manner. It is not an abstract lifeless theological formulation with little bearing on the life of the individual or the community. The Trinity for Panikkar is intricately bound up with the everyday experiences of both the ordinary person and those who dedicate their entire lives to the search for enlightenment and truth.

The Christology that Panikkar develops as seen especially in the first edition of his *The Unknown Christ of Hinduism* (1964) is also an attempt to show the universality of Christianity. His concept of "many Christs" is intended to capture the genuine religious experiences of those who worship or are drawn to and liberated spiritually by the Gods or religious figures of the great world religions. Panikkar's Christology, as it affects the further development of his concept of the Trinity, will be discussed *passim* in the remainder of this book.

To conclude: Panikkar's cosmotheandric vision, his awareness of the importance of the experience of the person as individual and communitarian, his consciousness of the importance of intrareligious dialogue, his ability to see beyond the normal Christian confines of the Trinity and his belief that Christianity was truly meant to be a universal religion have accounted for certain dynamics in his thought.

Three consequences emerge from Panikkar's particular methodology, that is, the keys and dynamics of his trinitarian thought. First, his trinitarian vision at the heart of the experience of the world religions both individually and collectively has given him the scope and flexibility to develop a concept of Trinity and a Christology with far reaching repercussions. Secondly, the accumulated knowledge of the world religions, especially regarding the "experiential" systems of the world religions, has enabled him to use new sets of terms and has allowed a radical reformulation of the concept of the Trinity. In the third place, by wrestling with this new trinitarian "vision" Panikkar has been able to probe even further into the core of these various religious systems and has offered further insight into the several strains of his thought.

There are three problems that emerge as a result of the keys and dynamics at work in Panikkar's thought. The problems follow upon his struggle with the parallel formulation of the two concepts of Trinity: one based on the Advaita Vedanta tradition alone and the other based on the various spiritualities of the world religions. The first problem becomes evident in the perception of his notion of "Christ," further complicated by the publication of the second edition of his *The Unknown Christ in Hinduism* (1981), which appears to break with the notion of fullness of revelation in Jesus Christ. Secondly, an additional complication occurs when Panikkar becomes fully familiar with the different stages of consciousness in Eastern religions and with the perception, experiences and relationship with the "Gods" or sacred figures of the East, whereas the Western Christian-centred readers are looking at the "Gods" from a historical or concretized perspective. Thirdly, because much of Panikkar's thought is not explained sufficiently for the Western mind and because the Western Christian reader is not able to experience the context out of which these "Gods" emerge and are revered, severe difficulties of understanding and interpretation arise.

C. Terminology

Panikkar's main contribution to trinitarian theology as well as Christology is closely connected with his use of terminology. There is a sense in which the development of his trinitarian thought is parallel to the development of his ablility to use terminology in a way that speaks of the experience of the Ultimate across religious and cultural boundaries. In a sense this entire work speaks of Panikkar's terminology.

First, this section will highlight some of the difficulties encountered by Panikkar with the use of language in the development of his thought on the Trinity. Secondly, it will also point out problems with using terminology from other religious traditions. Thirdly, it will indicate some of the original terminology that Panikkar adopts and to which he assigns meaning that is meant to be transcultural. Further explanations of his terminology are given throughout this work.

1. Difficulties Encountered

The task of applying such a specifically Christian concept as the Trinity to the world religions required careful attention to the terminology used in crossing over to various religions and cultures. Panikkar experienced the inadequacies of language and the need for new nomenclature to express himself as his thought developed over the years. At times, he claimed that he was misunderstood. "My book, *The Unknown Christ of Huiduism* (1964) was dedicated to the *Unknown Christ* as a parallel to Paul's 'Unknown God,' but was sometimes misunderstood to be speaking about the Christ known to Christians and unknown to Hindus . . ."[84]

Here the problem was not simply the misunderstanding of terminology. The trinitarian theology and the Christology that Panikkar was espousing not only was in the process of development but lacked clarity of expression primarily because the task that he was undertaking was extremely challenging. The language problem was further complicated because, as Panikkar explained, "Christian history has been forged by the unfolding of Christian belief against the background of Hebrew religion and Greek culture."[85] To describe Christian theology, and especially the Trinity, in a way that included the experience of Buddhists and Hindus with vastly different backgrounds required new language, symbols, metaphors and categories. Panikkar had to coin terminology throughout the development of his thought.

2. Terminology From Various Theological Schools

In his discussion of Hinduism, Panikkar is well aware of the problem of language. He remarks, "We have to recognize at the very outset that we do not (yet?) have a universal language."[86] It is not simply a matter of translating Sanskrit, Pali or Tibetan words into English, although this is complex in itself. It involves the complicated issue of prior assumptions and the meaning of symbols. Panikkar, although working with scientific theological data, is involved in a language, i.e. terminology, which originated from a milieu of assumptions that are different from the assumptions and language out of which Hindu religious texts, statements, categories and intuitions emerge.

In using language or terminology evolving from the Christian and Hindu traditions, Panikkar is well aware of the hermeneutical dilemma involved. He writes, "we need a common symbolics, not only to check the translation and to establish a two-way communication, but also to enable us even to make the translation."[87] He is keenly aware of the power of words and terms across cultures and especially within the different texts of the world religions.[88] It is this profound awareness that prompts him to examine words painstakingly in their context in order to acheive a deeper meaning or the specific point of view that he is trying to convey.

Panikkar also probes Hindu and Buddhist texts that employ Sanskrit and Pali words which often have no English equivalents. At times he settles for a literal translation. However, because the Western reader may not be familiar with the Eastern religious concepts, understanding his terminology becomes ever more arduous. The goal of existence for the Christian is union with God in Christ. This same goal, Panikkar claims, is expressed in other religious traditions by using varied terminology: "We have used the expression, 'union with the Absolute,' whereas a Yogin would prefer to say 'pure isolation' and a Buddhist, 'Nirvana.'"[89]

Panikkar uses such words as Sunyata and Pleroma in his discussion of the concept of the Ultimate in Buddhism. He states, "It would require an entire volume to render even cursorily the different interpretations of these central notions."[90] He then offers some explanation of their meaning. His interpretation of Eastern concepts tends in the direction of whatever resembles categories within the Christian tradition that can shed light on or deepen already existing concepts of the Ultimate.

Panikkar also borrows the concept of Nirvana from Buddhism. The use of this concept is central to the development of Panikkar's trinitarian theology. In his earlier thought he adapts this state of "consciousness" or experience to typify the spirituality that most resembles the "experience" of the First Person of the Trinity. It assisted him in the categorization of the experiences within the various spiritualities of the world religions. Besides the use of Nirvana in this general manner, Panikkar employs the concept of Nirvana to describe the concept of Father in all its non-expressions. These two uses of the term Nirvana, which frequently overlap, are employed throughout the development of his thinking. In his recent thought, especially when Panikkar concentrates on the Trinity as experienced in the secular world, this concept of Nirvana is almost non-existent. However, Panikkar never departs from saying that this category is important for the Christian experience of the Trinity, if that experience is to be brought to greater depth and experienced in truly universal dimensions.

Also crucial is Panikkar's use of the word Advaita. He uses the concept throughout the development of his thought on the Trinity. Although his trinitarian thought undergoes many twists and turns, he never abandons the concept of Advaita. In his consideration of each of the Three Persons of the Trinity, aspects of the Advaita tradition of Hinduism are utilized.

In his *The Unknown Christ of Hinduism* (both 1964 and 1981 editions), the complete Trinity with Isvara as the "Christ" is seen within the context of the Advaita tradition. In his specifically trinitarian work, *The Trinity and Religious Experience of Man*, the experience of Advaita (non-duality) is employed to typify the experience of the Holy Spirit. In his development of the Trinity, as envisioned within the secular world apart from all religious categories, Advaita is utilized in the "Atman equals Brahman" concept, where the Trinity is realized within the depth of the human person.

Although used extensively throughout his trinitarian works, the term Advaita is never really explored at any great depth. In his early works, the struggle to express what he means when using the Advaita tradition is evident. He wrestles with the term turiya, which is the fourth "state of consciousness" within the Advaita tradition. Translating the Mandukya Upanishad (verse VII), he states, turiya is "That which is neither inner knowledge nor outer knowledge, nor both simultaneously, is not pure undifferentiated knowledge, is invisible, unapproachable, impalpable, indefinable, unthinkable, unnamable, whose very essence consists of the experience of his own self."[91] In a subsequent edition, published three years later where the text is almost identical, Panikkar tries to improve his terminology to unpack further meaning encapsulated within the Advaita tradition. He translates the same verse; but his terminology changes, and the verse is expanded. He describes turiya as:

> That which is neither internal consciousness nor external consciousness, nor together; which does not consist solely in compact consciousness, which is neither conscious nor unconscious; which is invisible, unapproachable, impalpable, indefinable, unthinkable, unnameable, whose very essence consists of the experience of its own self; which absorbs all diversity, is tranquil and benign, without a second, which is what they call the fourth state - that is the atman. (Mandukya Upanishad, V.7).[92]

The word Advaita not only represents non-duality, but also an entire process and religious system that can never be completely expressed in words. To elucidate it for the Western reader is what Panikkar attempted in the development of his trinitarian theology.

3. Original Terminology

In the development of his trinitarian thought, Panikkar coins several words, often borrowing from various schools, to explain his thought. Throughout this work Panikkar's terminology will be elucidated to highlight the scope of meaning and the various dimensions that he wishes to assign to his terms in order that they may function either as probing tools or keys for bringing about new ways of thinking about the Triune God.

Panikkar coins words and phrases borrowed from various categories which are somewhat difficult to grasp. For example, "metaontological equivalence," which means the following:

I mean, by this, that all those concepts stand for the same Omega and that this Omega is more than just a mere name. I cannot say that this Omega exists, because the very word betrays a certain philosophical view. I cannot even say that it is, nor, on the other hand say that it is not. What I am trying to put across is that this is more than a simple formal device, that it is the reality of the human adventure, even if one thinks of it as being utter nothingness.[93]

He creates expressions such as "I-am-ness"[94] to express himself when explaining Eastern concepts.

There are several key terms that emerge in Panikkar's vocabulary. Some examples follow. In relation to Trinity, he uses words such as "Christ," which reflect a meaning or a multiplicity of meanings for the Christian within a definite parameter, to mean something significantly different. For instance, the title "Christ" for the Christian is attributed uniquely to Jesus. For Panikkar, "Christ" can be attributed also to Buddha, Isvara, Krishna, etc.

Another term that Panikkar employs in the context of Trinity is "cosmotheandrism." To this word he adds his own unique meaning.[95] As his concept of Trinity develops further, his notion of cosmotheandrism takes on greater importance.[96]

Still another term found in the development of Panikkar's trinitarian thought is "homeomorphic equivalent." In his earlier writings he had difficulty explaining that the Triune God was "equal" to Brahman or Allah, because equality was not considered an adequate word to describe what Panikkar was attempting to say. The problem deepened as Panikkar tried to explain that Jesus was equal to "Christ" but "Christ" was not equal to Jesus. "Christ" could also be experienced as Isvara, Siva, Buddha, etc. Borrowing from mathematics, Panikkar utilized the term "homeomorphic equivalent" to explain that it is not "equal" to, but "takes the place of," that which Christ represents for the Christian, however, immersed in a completely different context with another set of terms, symbols, religious language and culture. With regard to the term "Christ," Panikkar is speaking not only in terms of homeomorphic equivalence. He sees "his concept of the universal Christ" as unfolding the mystery of the "traditional Christian concept of the universal Christ" by elucidating the experience of God (Ultimate) in the context of Isvara, Siva, Buddha, as well as other "Christs." Panikkar's use of the term "homeomorphic equivalent" is not limited to his later trinitarian thought, but permeates most of his writings.

Throughout the development of his trinitarian thought still another term surfaces: "christophany." The word and the meaning given to it by Panikkar indicates, not so much a change in his thinking, but rather a reinforcement and development of his thought, as expressed in the 1992 "Cardinal Bellarmine Lecture."[97] For Panikkar, each person is a christophany. Each person is a "manifestation of the christic adventure of all reality on its way towards infinite mystery."[98] The Trinity is fully manifested through the universal Christ[99] and every human being shares intimately in that journey towards an evolution that is similiar to the Advaita concept in which Atman equals Brahman.

Panikkar's terminology is further complicated by his tendency to hyphenate words, to favor inverted commas, to break up sentences beyond the normal usage and frequently to borrow from Eastern languages in a style that is fluid but elusive at the same time. In general, Panikkar's terminology, although it is meant to elucidate, often results in a style that is both complex and difficult to comprehend. M.M. Thomas in his Foreword to Panikkar's *The Trinity and World Religions* remarks, "The book *is* difficult reading, because the concepts are complex and certain key words used in it are unfamiliar. The complexity is perhaps inherent in Panikkar's background - linquistic, philosophical and theological."[100]

Notes

1   Ignatius Hirudayam, "My Spiritual Journey Through the Highways and Byways of Interreligious Dialogue," in *Interreligious Dialogue: Voices From a New Frontier*, ed. M. Darrol Bryant and Frank Flinn (New York: Paragon House, 1989), 62.

2   Panikkar, *Trinity and Religious Experience*, vii.

3   For evidence of this in relation to the Third World see material from the EATWOT Conferences (1976-1983), especially Virginia Fabella and Sergio Torres, eds., *Irruption of the Third World* (Maryknoll: Orbis Books, 1983) and *Doing Theology in a Divided World* (Maryknoll: Orbis Books, 1985). Also see Secretariatus Pro Non-Christianis, *For a Dialogue With Hinduism* (Rome: Editrice Ancora, Date not given); John Paul II, *The Mission of Christ the Redeemer. Encyclical Letter. Redemptoris Missio*, December 7, 1990 (Sherbrooke, Quebec: Éditions Paulines, 1991). English translation by the Vatican (*Redemptoris Missio, Acta Apostolicae Sedis* 83 [1991], 249-340).

4   See Paul F. Knitter, *No Other Name? A Critical Survey of Christian Attitudes Towards the World Religion* (Maryknoll: Orbis Books, 1985).

5   For example, John Hick and Paul Knitter, eds., *The Myth of Christian Uniqueness: Toward a Pluralistic Theology of Religions* (Maryknoll: Orbis Books, 1987).

6   Joseph Cardinal Ratzinger and Vittorio Messori, *The Ratzinger Report,* trans. Salvator Attanasio and Graham Harrison (San Francisco: Ignatius Press, 1985), 197.

7   *Ibid.*

8   Raimundo Panikkar "The Category of Growth in Comparative Religion: A Critical Self-Examination," *Harvard Theological Review* 66 (1973): 130. A similar article under the same title was reprinted in Raimundo Panikkar, *The Intrareligious Dialogue* (New York: Paulist Press, 1978), 53-75. Later Panikkar emerges with a more forceful position. See Raimundo Panikkar "Is History the Measure of Man?" *The Teilhard Review* 16 (1981): 39-45.

9   See Ovey Mohammed, "Commentary on the Declaration on the Relationship of the Church to Non-Christian Religions *Nostra Aetate,*" *The Documents of Vatican II Reconsidered*, ed. G.P. Schner (New York: University Press of America, 1986), 141. See also Paul Knitter, *Toward a Protestant Theology of Religions* (Marburg: N.G. Elwert, 1974), 230; Paul Knitter "Roman Catholic Approaches to Other Religions: Developments and Tensions," *International Bulletin of Missionary Research* 8 (1984): 50-54. See also Hick and Knitter, eds. *The Myth of Christian Uniqueness*, 82, 178-197.

10   Mohammed, "Commentary on the Declaration on the Relationship of the Church to Non-Christian Religions," 141.

11   John Moffitt, "Christianity Confronts Hinduism," *Theological Studies* 30 (1969), 208.

12   Karl Rahner, *The Trinity*, trans. Joseph Donceel (New York: Herder and Herder, 1970), 10-11.

13   Advaita means non-duality, unitive life, communion of the soul with God. This Vedanta philosophical system teaches the ultimate oneness of Brahman, embodied souls (jivas) and the universe (jaqat) together with the unreality of the last two apart from Brahman. Gaudapada and Sankaracharya are the main and classic exponents of the Advaita system.

14   For a concise, simplified and yet comprehensive version of Buddhism see Walpola Rahula, *What the Buddha Taught* (New York: Grove Press, 1974).

15   Panikkar, *Unknown Christ of Hinduism* (1981), 67, n. 14.

16   Panikkar, "The Category of Growth in Comparative Religion," 131. See also Raimundo Panikkar "In Christ There is Neither Hindu nor Christian: Perspectives on Hindu-Christian Dialogue," in *Religious Issues* and *Interreligious Dialogues*, ed. C. Wei-hsun Fu and G.E. Spiegler (New York: Greenwood Press, 1989), 475-489.

17   Panikkar, "In Christ There Is Neither Hindu nor Christian," 482.

18   See Panikkar, *Intrareligious Dialogue*, 68.

19   John Macquarrie, *Principles of Christian Theology,* 2nd ed. (New York: Charles Scribner's Sons, 1977), 4-18.

20   *Ibid.*, 4-5.

21   *Ibid.*, 5.

23   Panikkar, "The Category of Growth in Comparative Religion," 116.

24   Panikkar, "In Christ There Is Neither Hindu nor Christian," 481.

25   Macquarrie, *Principles of Christian Theology*, 7.

26   *Ibid.*

27   *Ibid.*, 11.

28   *Ibid.*, 12.

29   *Ibid.*, 13.

30   Ewert Cousins, "Raimundo Panikkar and the Christian Systematic Theology of the Future," *Cross Currents* 29 (1979): 148.

31   See Panikkar, *Unknown Christ of Hinduism* (1981), 148.

32   Macquarrie, *Principles of Christian Theology*, 14.

34   John S. Dunne, *The Way of All the Earth: Experiments in Truth and Religion* (New York : MacMillan Press, 1972), ix-x.

35   Raimundo Panikkar, "Instead of a Foreword: An Open Letter," in Dominic Veliath, *Theological Approach and Understanding of Religions: Jean Daniélou and Raimundo Panikkar, A Study in Contrast* (Bangalore: Kristu Jyoti College, 1988), xi. Letter written Easter 1987 in Tavertet.

36   Ewert Cousins, "Introduction: The Panikkar Symposium at Santa Barbara," *Cross Currents* 29 (1979): 131.

37   Macquarrie, *Principles of Christian Theology*, 18.

38   *Ibid.*

39   *Ibid.*, 16.

40   *Ibid.*

41   *Ibid.*, 17.

42   See *ibid.*

43   Panikkar, "The Radical Trinity" in *Gifford Lectures*, No.6.

44   See *ibid.*

45   See *ibid.*

46   Melchior Cano's classic work on theological sources and arguments, *De locis theologicis* (1563), enumerates ten *loci*, among which the magisterium plays an important part. See F. Courtney, "Cano Melchior," *New Catholic Encyclopedia* III, 28-29.

47   See Vatican Council II's Dogmatic Constitution on the Church, *Lumen Gentium*, 20-25; Vatican Council II's Dogmatic Constitution on Divine Revelation, *Dei Verbum*, 10.

48   See Robert Coffy, "The Magisterium and Theology," *Irish Theological Quarterly* 43 (1976): 247-259; "Cooperation between Theologians and the Ecclesiastical Magisterium," in *A Report of the Joint Committee of the Canon Law Society of America and the Catholic Theological Society of America*, ed. Leo O'Donovan(Washington, D.C.: Catholic University of America, 1982); "Instructio De Eccesiali Theologi Vocatione," Congregatio De Doctrina Fidei, *Acta Apostolicae Sedis* 82 (1990): 1550-1570. English translation, "Instruction on the Ecclesial Vocation of the Theologian," *Origins* 20 (1990): 117-126.

49   The official Latin text, with commentary by the two theologions most involved in drafting the theses, Otto Semmelroth and Karl Lehmann, is published in *Gregorianum*, 57 (1976), 549-563. English translation and commentary in Francis A. Sullivan, *Magisterium. Teaching Authority in the Catholic Church* (New York: Paulist Press, 1983), 174-218. (Quotations from the document will be taken from this translation.) In addition to the aforementioned commentary by Sullivan the following commentaries have also been consulted: Otto Semmelroth and Karl Lehmann, "Commentary on the Theses," published by the Publication Office, USCC, 1977, and reprinted in *Readings in Moral Theology No.3, The Magisterium and Morality*, eds. C.E. Curran and R.A. McCormick (New York: Paulist Press, 1982), 160-170; Stephen Happel, "Theologian," *New Catholic Encyclopedia*, Vol.17, 1979, 650.

50   Sullivan, *Magisterium*, 174.

51   Happel, "Theologian," 650.

52   See Panikkar, *The Unknown Christ of Hinduism*, 129.

53   Sullivan, *Magisterium*, 193.

54   Neither Cano nor Macquarrie include liturgy in their list of theological *loci*. Contemporary theologians fault Cano and others for this omission. See Gerald O'Collins and Edward Farrugia, *A Concise Dictionary of Theology* (New York: Paulist Press, 1991): 123 and 128.

55   "The study of sacred liturgy ... in theological faculties is to rank among the
      principal subjects ... Moreover, other professors, while striving to expound
      the mystery of Christ and the history of salvation ... must nevertheless do
      so in a way which will clearly bring out the connection between their subjects
      and the liturgy ... This consideration is especially important for professors
      of dogmatic, spiritual, and pastoral theology and holy Scripture," n.16. All
      quotations from Vatican Council II documents in this book are taken from
      the Walter Abbott translation, *The Documents of Vatican II. In a New and
      Definitive Translation with Commentaries and Notes by Catholic, Protestant
      and Orthodox Authorities*, Walter M. Abbott, General Editor (New York:
      Herder and Herder, 1966).

56   See O'Collins - Farrugia, *Concise Dictionary of Theology*, 123.

57   Avery Dulles, "Faith and Revelation," in *Systematic Theology. Roman
      Catholic Perspectives* I, ed. F.S. Fiorenza and J.P. Galvin (Minneapolis:
      Fortress Press, 1991), 122.

58   The fuller form is "legem credendi lex statuat supplicandi" and dates from
      St. Prosper of Aquitaine (d. ca. 463): *Enchiridion Symbolorum* ..., ed. H.
      Denzinger, A. Schönmetzer (Barcelona: Herder, 1976, 36th ed.), 246.

59   See Aidan Kavanagh, *On Liturgical Theology* (New York: Pueblo, 1984),
      esp. 88-95; also Edward J. Kilmartin, *Systematic Theology of Liturgy*, Vol.
      I of *Christian Liturgy: Theology and Practice* (Kansas City: Sheed and
      Ward, 1988), 96-99.

60   See Cyprian Vagaggini, *The Theological Dimensions of the Liturgy*
      (Collegeville: Liturgical Press, 1976), 4th ed., trans. L. Doyle and W.A.
      Jurgens. For example, there is a section on "The general Christological-
      Trinitarian perspective in the liturgy," 69-95.

61   See Yves M.J. Congar, *Je Crois en l'Esprit Saint, III: Le Fleuve de Vie
      coule, en Orient et en Occident* (Paris: Les Éditions du Cérf, 1980), *passim*.
      Trans. *I Believe in the Holy Spirit, III* (New York: Seabury Press; London:
      G. Chapman; 1983).

62   Aidan Nichols, *The Shape of Catholic Theology. An Introduction to Its
      Sources, Principles, and History* (Collegeville: Liturgical Press, 1991),
      187.

63   See Raimundo Panikkar, *Worship and Secular Man. An essay on the
      liturgical nature of Man, considering Secularization as a major phenomenon
      of our time and Worship as an apparent fact of all times. A study towards
      an integral anthropology* (Maryknoll: Orbis Books, 1973).

64   In his earlier works Panikkar uses the term "theandrism." In his later works,
      "cosmotheandrism" predominates.

65   Panikkar, *Trinity and World Religions*, 69.

66   *Ibid.*, 70.

67   For further development of the concept of theandrism see Raimundo
      Panikkar, "*Colligite Fragmenta*: For an Integration of Reality," in *From*

Alienation to At-one-ness, ed. F.A. Eigo (Philadelphia: Villanova University Press, 1977), 16, 19, especially 68-91. This thought is further developed in the *Gifford Lectures*, No. 7, entitled "The Cosmotheandric Invariant."

68   Panikkar is sometimes challenged in this area where the distinction between "the discovery of the self (Self?) ... [and] the encounter with the living God (god?)" becomes problematic. See Panikkar, "Instead of a Foreword: An Open Letter," v.

69   Panikkar, *Trinity and World Religions*, 73.

70   Swami Nikhilananda, trans., *The Upanishads* (New York: Harper Torchbooks, 1963), 164.

71   *Ibid.*, 161.

72   Panikkar, *Trinity and World Religions*, 73. Dharmakaya refers to one of the bodies of the Buddha as understood within the Mahayana School of Buddhism.

73   Panikkar, "Instead of a Foreword: An Open Letter," xii.

74   Frank Podgorski, "Toward the Convergence of Religious Experience," *Cross Currents* 29 (1979): 233.

75   *Ibid.*, 231.

76   Panikkar, *Intrareligious Dialogue*, 11.

77   *Ibid.*, 10.

78   *Ibid.*

79   Panikkar, "In Christ There Is Neither Hindu nor Christian," 475.

80   *Ibid.*

81   Panikkar, *Intrareligious Dialogue*, 11.

82   Panikkar, *Trinity and Religious Experience*, 71-72.

83   For Panikkar's categories of spiritualities, see Panikkar, *Trinity and Religious Experience*, 9-40.

84   Panikkar, "A Christophany for Our Times," 11.

85   *Ibid.*, 5.

86   Raimundo Panikkar, "The Silence of the Word : Non-dualistic Polarities," *Cross Currents* 29 (1974): 154.

87   Panikkar, "The Category of Growth in Comparative Religion," 132. See also Raymond Panikkar, *Myth, Faith and Hermeneutics* (New York: Paulist Press, 1979), especially 20-22, 191, 239, 322-455.

88   For a detailed explanation of Panikkar's use of words and their meaning see Raimundo Panikkar, "Words and Terms," in *Esistenza, Mito, Ermeneutica*, ed. M.M. Olivetti (Rome: Istituto di Studi Filosofici, 1980), 117 - 133.

89   Panikkar, *Unknown Christ of Hinduism* (1964), 5.

90   Panikkar, *The Intrareligious Dialogue*, 81. See also T.R.V. Murti, *The Central Philosophy of Buddhism* (London: George Allen and Unwin, 1960), 231-236.

91   Panikkar, *Trinity and World Religions* (1970), 34.

92   Panikkar, *Trinity and Religious Experience* (1973), 34.

93   Panikkar, "The Category of Growth in Comparative Religion," 134.

94   See Panikkar, *Myth, Faith and Hermeneutics*, 368.

95   See Panikkar, *Trinity and Religious Experience*, 71-82. See also, Panikkar, *Unknown Christ of Hinduism* (1981), 93-94.

96   See Panikkar, *"Colligite Fragmenta*: For an Intergration of Reality," 63, 68.

97   See Panikkar, "A Christophany for Our Times," 3-21. For an example of his earlier thought on the term christophany, see Panikkar, *Trinity and World Religions*, 53.

98   Panikkar, "A Christophany for Our Times," 20.

99   "Christ" is used in Panikkar's peculiar sense.

100 Panikkar, *Trinity and World Religions* (1970), viii.

Chapter II

The Earlier Panikkar on Trinity (1964-75)

Introduction

This chapter will examine the earlier thought of Raimon Panikkar on Trinity. Section A will explore Panikkar's trinitarian thought, especially in the context of the Christ experience within the Advaita school of Hinduism. Section B will continue to examine his earlier thought as he attempts to expand and deepen his concept of Trinity in the context of Christianity, Hinduism and Buddhism. Section C will explore other works of Panikkar pertinent to his earlier trinitarian thought. Section D will summarize his earlier trinitarian thought.

The dates of Panikkar's published main works on the Trinity are somewhat misleading. The reason is that he has a tendency to write material which is later published in the form of either articles or books with as much as a ten-year lag.[1] To complicate matters further, Panikkar at times takes already published articles and includes them later as sections within newly published books. Because he writes in several languages, with English as the primary one, identical or near identical texts are further duplicated into other languages, bearing a wide range of publication dates.

The two principal texts used in this chapter to reflect his earlier trinitarian thought are *The Unknown Christ of Hinduism* (1964) and *The Trinity and the Religious Experience of Man* (1973). The main reason for using *The Unknown Christ of Hinduism* (1964), rather than numerous articles from the early 1960's to 1973, is that it gives a concise account of Panikkar's attempt to view the Trinity within the Advaita religious system. Because the first Foreword was written in 1957, it can be identified as his earliest work.[2] It provides a basis for his trinitarian thought, although it is primarily christological.

The Trinity and the Religous Experience of Man (1973) has been selected to represent another aspect of Panikkar's earlier thought, although it was published in 1973 after his two earlier English works, that is, his article "Toward an Ecumenical Theandric Spirituality," published in 1968, and the Madras edition of his book, *The Trinity and World Religions*, published in 1970. All of these texts are almost identical in content, except for the Preface and Foreword and some very minor points. *The Trinity and the Religious Experience of Man* (1973) is the principal reference; any departure from material published earlier is carefully documented. Also, the 1970 edition of *The Trinity and World Religions* (1970) is out of print and not easily accessible.

In Panikkar's earliest thought on the Trinity, a definite Christian perspective is adhered to. He treats of the Trinity from the perspective of a Christian convinced of its potential to speak truly of the Godhead beyond Christian parameters while retaining the authentic teachings of the Catholic church on the dogma of the Trinity.

In *The Unknown Christ of Hinduism* (1964), Panikkar attempts to show that the Hindu view of the Absolute and the Lord Isvara foreshadows the Christian trinitarian doctrine. In this work, Panikkar is trying to reflect the Godhead found in Vedantic Scriptures and Vedantic terminology and to show parallels between Hinduism and Christianity.

The other principal text used in this present chapter, *The Trinity and the Religious Experience of Man* (1973), deals more directly with the Trinity, but in a way that combines spiritualities and diverse experiences of "God" (Ultimate) from the Buddhist, Christian and Hindu (Advaita) traditions and links these to the experience of Father, Son and the Holy Spirit, respectively. The work itself, although noteworthy in bringing forth new dimensions of the Trinity from a truly universal perspective, is far from adequate in dealing with the emerging questions surrounding the historical Jesus as revealer of the Blessed Trinity.

Panikkar's text *The Unknown Christ of Hinduism* (1964), although published earlier than his specifically trinitarian work, *The Trinity and the Religious Experience of Man* (1973), provides insights into the way he formulates his trinitarian thought. In this text, Isvara in Advaita takes the place of Jesus in Christianity, without Jesus being disclaimed as the fullness of revelation. Therefore, Isvara becomes the Revealer of the Trinity in Advaita.

The two principal sections of the chapter (A and B) will examine these two works in relation to the Trinity. Although *The Unknown Christ of Hinduism* (1964) reflects his earlier thought according to the dates that are available, nevertheless, it appears that there are two parallel formulations of the Trinity central to the thought of the earlier Panikkar. First, there is the Trinity seen within the parameters of the Advaita tradition. This perspective can then be extrapolated to any other non-Christian religious system. Secondly, there is the Trinity seen as the experience of God reflected through various spiritualities: Buddhism; Advaita in Hinduism; and Christianity.

A. *First Edition of* The Unknown Christ of Hinduism *(1964)*

In *The Unknown Christ of Hindusim* (1964) Panikkar proceeds with an insightful premise. Since there is only one universal God, who is the Triune God, this Triune God must be present within the concept of Brahman, the all-embracing God of Hindusim. The immediate difficulty faced by Panikkar is: How can the Three Persons of the Trinity be equated with Braham, who is described as God with two aspects, Nirguna Brahman and Saguna Brahman?

First, Panikkar decides to equate Nirguna Brahman with the Father. However, he does so with some ambiguity. Secondly, Panikkar makes a connection between the Christian concept of Christ and that of Saguna Brahman, who is Brahman manifested in the world. Thirdly, he envisions a connection between the Holy Spirit in Christianity and the experience of non-duality in the Advaita tradition.

In this text, Panikkar views the Trinity as Father, Logos and Holy Spirit: "I believe . . . (i)n God, so my faith unfolds it, Who is Trinity - Father, Logos and Holy Spirit."[3] He expands this further: "And again faith will let me into the unfathomable womb of the divinity and make me discover, realize, that this father is all-powerful, creator . . . and the Logos became man . . . and the Spirit breathes in his Church. . ."[4]

There is a struggle in Panikkar's earlier thought to arrive at a description or descriptions of the Trinity (Godhead). The operative dynamic throughout this work is to achieve a description of God, the Trinity, that is authentic from a Christian perspective as well as one from the viewpoint of the Advaita Vedanta tradition.

In the section of the book entitled "Advaita and Trinity,"[5] this difficulty from the Indian perspective is clearly seen. The Trinity in Vedantic terminology becomes problematic in the relationship between "Brahman, the Absolute, the Transcendent, the Unknown and . . . Isvara, the Lord, the Creator, the God."[6] The problem is very complex because in Advaita, the Godhead can barely be spoken of as distinct from the rest of reality. The Mandukya Upanishad thus describes God:

> HARIH AUM! AUM, the word, is all this. All that is past, present and future is, indeed, Aum. And whatever else there is, beyond the threefold division of time - that also is truly Aum. All this is indeed, Brahman. This Atman is Brahman.[7]

Panikkar sees the Trinity as the possible solution to the Indian[8] question of the relationship of God with the world, the absolute with the relative. He states, "the dogma of the Trinity would appear as the unsought for - and often indeed inopportune - answer to the inevitable question of an ontic mediator between the one and the manifold, the absolute and the relative, Brahman and this world."[9] Along with this prevailing difficulty, Panikkar is attempting a synthesis of the Trinity from two diverse traditions.

1. First Person of the Trinity

Panikkar's trinitarian thought, developed within the Advaita Vedanta tradition, situates God the Father as "the Source of the whole Divinity."[10] For Panikkar the Father is also the One to whom all of creation returns.[11]

At times Panikkar uses the term "God" in this early text (1964),[12] when he really means "Father." This will be evident in the revised edition (1981),[13] where he changes the word "God" to "Father." In this early text, the concept of the Father in the Trinity is not as explicit as in his later works. Yet one is already able to discern in these early texts hints of later developments from "God" to "Father." In the Advaita tradition, God is expressed as follows: "There is Brahman, or God, or the godhead as the absolute and in consequence unrelated, unchangeable, unique, simple - really *nirguna*."[14] It is this concept of God that Panikkar later assigns to the Father.

In the following section, which treats of the Second Person of the Trinity in this same work, *The Unknown Christ of Hinduism* (1964), even more is conveyed about the Father implicitly, as Panikkar develops his concept of Christ. In the First Person of the Trinity, there is no manifestation, no multiplicity, no appearance. The Father is silent, inacessible, the source of the whole Divinity. He is the source of all that there is. Yet to speak of the First Person of the Trinity alone makes no sense. Nothing can be said of Him except through the Son:

> *That from which all things proceed and to which all things return and by which all things are* (sustained in their own being) that 'that' is God, but *primo et per se* not a silent Godhead, not a kind of inaccessible Brahman, not God the Father and the source of the whole Divinity, but the true Isvara, God the Son, the Logos, the Christ.[15]

To summarize this section on the First Person of the Trinity: Panikkar makes a connection between the First Person of the Trinity and Nirguna Brahman. However, since Panikkar views the major connection between Christianity and Hindusim as hinging upon his own concept of "Christ," whom he identifies with Saguna Brahman, he proceeds to develop, instead of a trinitarian theology, a Christology that is at this point of his thought still in keeping with traditional Christian theology. This he does at the expense of his concept of the Father which remains somewhat undeveloped in this earlier work. Nevertheless, some aspects of Panikkar's trinitarian thought in relation to the First Person of the Trinity are in evidence. First, the Father is the source of the whole divinity. Secondly, the Father appears as having all the attributes of Nirguna Brahman. Thirdly, the Father is not described in terms of person. In this early work the concept of the Father is ambiguous and somewhat undifferentiated.

2. Second Person of the Trinity

This section will deal with the correspondence between the Second Person of the Trinity and Saguna Brahman (God with appearance). The section will depict Panikkar as seemingly to be moving away from the Trinity. His focus becomes a Christology with emphasis on the concept of Isvara. In spite of the fact that it is mainly a Christology, it is crucial to his trinitarian thought. It is in his struggle to present a universal "Christ" that Panikkar explores thoroughly the concept of Isvara in the Advaita tradition of Hinduism and in so doing embarks upon a new trinitarian theology.

In the earlier Panikkar, the Second Person of the Trinity is seen as "Isvara, God the Son, the Logos, the Christ."[16] Even though Panikkar tries to formulate the Trinity from the Advaita tradition,[17] what really emerges is a focusing on Isvara as the Christ. Section (a) below will briefly outline how Panikkar develops his thought on Isvara. It will be descriptive. Section (b), which is more important, will show some of the factors at work in this early text that attempt to mesh together the two perspectives of the Trinity: the Christian and the Advaitin.

a) Isvara as Christ

In his attempt to develop a trinitarian concept with its "christological" Isvara, Panikkar makes three statements from a Hindu perspective. First, there is Brahman, God as Absolute, that is, without relation.[18] Secondly, there is the world consisting of Gods, human beings and "gross" matter with all the attributes which, however, cannot be associated with Nirguna Brahman, such as manifestation, multiplicity and appearance.[19] Thirdly, there is need for a relation or link of cause and mediator between Brahman and the world, because "if there is *no* link, the dualism that thus arises destroys both Brahman and the World."[20]

It is Isvara that provides the link. Isvara is the Lord, the Personal God and Creator, who is Saguna[21] Brahman or Brahman conditioned by maya.[22] Isvara in Panikkar's thought is not a secondary Saguna Brahman.[23] Isvara is identified with the "only one Source, only one ultimate Reality, but yet it is distinct from it, for it is its 'expression,' its image, its 'revealer.'"[24]

Panikkar limits his discussion of the function of Isvara[25] to Vedantic theology and presents the role of Isvara in the Vedanta school in a general manner. Panikkar argues that, although Brahman is the absolute and unique cause of the universe, Isvara still enjoys a fundamental place for seven reasons.[26] 1. Isvara provides the possibility of relations because Brahman is devoid of relations. Isvara is "existence, consciousness and bliss in the relational ense."[27] 2. Because Brahman cannot be a person, Isvara is the personal aspect of Brahman.[28]

3. Because of Brahman's absolute transcendence, as such He cannot be creator of the world. Therefore, Isvara is responsible for the creation of the world.[29] 4. Because Brahman cannot be made responsible for the

SIE

7533

30516022138803

Pickup By: 10/19/2018

A critical reading of the development of

PLEASE CHECKOUT ITEM

~

return of the world to its origin and its reality, Isvara must function as grace towards the realization of Brahman. 5. Through the grace of Isvara and because of their identification with Him, the souls of living beings grow in their awareness that there is Brahman. Isvara is the link to a realization of what really is.[30] 6. Isvara has to perform the functions in relation to the universe and to souls because Brahman is immutable and unmanifest. Brahman is beyond all capacity for action; hence, the need for Isvara, who sometimes manifests Himself as many *avatars*.[31] 7. Finally, Isvara preserves both the transcendence and immanence of Brahman because He does all for Brahman. He is distinct from Brahman because He is the creative and manifested presence of Brahman but is also in Oneness with Brahman and in one way or another identical to Brahman.[32]

According to Panikkar, "Whatever kind of reality this temporal world may have, it is also sustained, conditioned, produced and attracted by this divine mediator."[33] Panikkar boldly asserts, quoting in part from the *Brahma-Sutra, "that from which this world comes forth and to which it returns and by which it is sustained, that,* 'that' is Christ."[34]

b) Significant Factors in Panikkar's Early Christology

In the Christology of Panikkar's early thought, the fullness of revelation is seen in Jesus and in the Christ Event. In fact, emphasis is given to the Eucharist: "Simply because Christ is fully present in the eucharist and the eucharist has been entrusted to the Church, Hinduism also has a right to have it, which comes to mean that Christianity has not the right to keep it for itself, but must offer it even to the Hindu."[35]

This fullness is brought out again in the following text:

> By its very nature Christianity presents itself as the catholic religion, as the full and universal religion. Not only God's will, but also the fact that this very will has shaped so the nature of Christianity, prevents us from considering it as *one* religion among others, or even as a *prima inter pares*. Christianity is the fullness of religion and thus the real per-fection of every religion.[36]

Panikkar is saying that Christ is fully manifested in Jesus Christ and that His Real Presence is embodied in the Eucharist and given in its entirety to the Church to be made known to the whole world. In this very early work, although little is said about the Sacraments, they are very much a concern for Panikkar. He still sees the Sacraments as the visible manifestations of Jesus Christ.

At the same time the Sacraments constitute one of the key problems of the Christian-Hindu encounter. In fact, Panikkar views the main problems of the Christian-Hindu encounter to be the "problems of time, creation and the sacraments."[37] In addition to the Sacraments being central to Christianity, Panikkar has to deal with a concept of Christ that must take into account "time" and "creation," concepts that are on opposite poles in the Christian and Hindu traditions. Although he does not resolve the problem in this text, he is fully aware of it. It surfaces dramatically in his later works and permeates his latest thought on the Trinity.

Because Panikkar moves away significantly, although in a very subtle way, from his position on Christ and Christianity, it is important to examine at least briefly his goal, the background, as he states it, and the evaluation of his own relation to traditional Christianity.

In the earliest text that clearly states his Christology, Panikkar thus descibes his goal: "The *goal* of this study . . . is an attempt to arrive at a certain understanding without renouncing any of the specific Christian truths, without levelling down Christianity to mere natural apologetics, but presenting the full Christian doctrine in all its glaring exigency."[38]

Panikkar summarizes the background as follows: "The *background* is on the one hand the horizon of the world-religions, especially the luxuriant world of Hinduism, and on the other hand the present day mentality of Christian and non-Christian scholars dealing with general problems of philosophy and religion."[39] Although Panikkar focuses on the Advaita Vedanta tradition in the development of his Christology, his thought embraces a much wider background.

As for Panikkar's evalution of his own relation to traditional Christianity, he is aware that he is moving away somewhat from traditional Christian approaches in the formulation of his Christology: "The author believes that his thesis flows almost evidently from the traditional Christian doctrine, but this does not mean that it should be the only possible one."[40]

To summarize this section on the Second Person of the Trinity: In this early work *The Unknown Christ of Hindusim* (1964) Panikkar's concept of Christ the Logos is elucidated within the Advaita tradition of Hinduism. Although "Christ" is seen manifested in Hinduism (Advaita) in the form of Isvara, "Christ" is still a hidden Christ. It is only in

Christianity that the Second Person of the Trinity is manifested in his fullness through the historical Jesus. The following are the conclusions of Panikkar in his formulation of "Christ" in Hinduism. First, "Christ" is experienced as Isvara in the Advaita tradition. Secondly, although not stated explicitly, "Christ" as Isvara in the Advaita tradition fulfills the role of Saguna Brahman in Hinduism. Thirdly, in the process of presenting "Christ" as Saguna Brahman, Panikkar reinterprets both Hindu doctrine and traditional Christian theology. Fourthly, Panikkar affirms the full presence of Christ in the Eucharist. Fifthly, he also affirms Christianity as the fullness of religion and the perfection of every religion. Sixthly, Panikkar extrapolates from the concept of "Isvara as the Christ" to the understanding that there are many "manifestations of Christ" in the various world religions. In this work Panikkar's concept of the Second Person of the Trinity is riddled with problems of clarity. The primary reason is that Panikkar does not deal adequately with the historical Jesus in relation to these "other manifestations of Christ" which are seen within a "transhistorical" context. Also, it is unclear how Panikkar can equate "Christ" with Saguna Brahman in a way that is acceptable not only to traditional Christian theology but even to traditional Hindu thought.

3. Third Person of the Trinity

The Holy Spirit is described in Panikkar's *The Unknown Christ of Hinduism* (1964) in very traditional Pneumatology. In the process of attempting to reconstruct a new Christology Panikkar presents a very brief final section entitled "Advaita and the Trinity," with fleeting glimpses of the Holy Spirit. From the Christian perspective the following traditional points are noted in this work.

a) Panikkar views the Holy Spirit as one of the Three Persons of the Trinity. The Trinity is "Father, Logos and Holy Spirit" in terminology that is basically still traditionally Christian.[41]

b) Whatever is done in Christ, the Spirit is there to hasten it: "In him all is recapitulated and the Spirit will quicken it with that life which overflows out of the father alone."[42]

c) In the 1957 first Foreword of this 1964 text of *The Unknown Christ of Hinduism*, Panikkar refers to the Holy Spirit as the one who inspires, who speaks: "only the Holy Spirit inspires the words of his living witnesses, and He takes

care to tell us not to premeditate what we are going to say
or how we are going to present the message."[43] Also for
Panikkar ". . . the mind guided by the Spirit, traces words
in the pure hearts of those who listen. . . . 'And they shall
be all taught of God' [Jn 6: 45] . . ."[44] For Panikkar the
Holy Spirit is active in his whole being, guiding him towards
Truth and the expression of that Truth. His reflection on
the Holy Spirit, as well as his entire trinitarian thought, is
not just an academic formulation. It involves his own
participation and growth.

d) In the thought of the earlier Panikkar, which is still very
traditional, "the Spirit breathes in his Church."[45] It is
because the Spirit breathes in his Church that the Church is
so special. The Christian Church enjoys, or is called to, a
special existence because of the Holy Spirit who is received
at Baptism. "One has to be reborn in water, blood and
Holy Spirit to the new Christian existence."[46]

In this volume of extensive bridge-building between Christianity
and Hinduism, the concept of the Holy Spirit plays an important part. It
is true that Panikkar often refers to Christ as the point of encounter
between Christianity and Hinduism, as seen in the following text:
"Christianity and Hinduism both meet in Christ. Christ is their meeting
point."[47] Although in this text there is an emphasis on the meeting point
being in Christ, later in the book Panikkar declares that it is in the Spirit
that the meeting of spiritualities between Christianity and Hinduism takes
place: "The meeting of spiritualities can only take place in the Spirit.
No new 'system' has primarily to come out of this encounter, but a new
and yet old *spirit* must emerge."[48] It is the Spirit which brings forth that
which is good from past and present, synthesizing it, bringing about a
new spirit, a newness that brings about an ever awakening Reality.

In this volume Panikkar includes a final thirteen page section entitled
"Advaita and Trinity." One would expect some development of the theme.
However, this section was written before 1961[49] and progresses very
little beyond traditional Catholic Pneumatology.

To summarize: In this work Panikkar presents a Pneumatology from
the viewpoint of traditional trinitarian thought. In addition to referring
to the Holy Spirit as a bridge-builder between Christianity and Hinduism,
little else is offered.

B. The Trinity and the Religious Experience of Man (1973)

In this work Panikkar grapples with the fact that the doctrine of Trinity is not completely adequate in its presentation, not only to Christians, but also to the rest of the world, especially to adherents of the other religions. To Christians, it is primarily a theoretical statement that is rarely experiential. To adherents of other religions, it is solely a Christian dogma that has very little relevance, if any, for the lives of non-Christians.

Panikkar is convinced that the Trinity is a truly universal phenomenon which transcends the realm of theoretical Christian dogma. This conviction prompts him to analyze the Trinity in the context of the world religions.

In terms of universality Panikkar begins his discussion of the Trinity with a consideration of experience, the first of the formative factors of theology. The experience of God or of the Divine, of that which is beyond all expression, for Panikkar is the experience of the Blessed Trinity. Therefore, he sets out in search of the experience of the Trinity within the context of the other world religions. In Hinduism he explores the Advaita Vedanta experience as well as the Bhakti experience. In Buddhism he considers the Nirvana experience as important in developing a further aspect of the Trinity. Reasoning from the basic premise that whenever God or the Divine is experienced within a religious system, the Trinity itself is experienced, Panikkar introduces a new dimension into his trinitarian thought.

He points out that the three basic forms of spirituality in Hinduism and Buddhism, that is, iconolatry, personalism and knowledge/mysticism, can be reconciled and synthesized through the concept of the Trinity. In this aspect of his trinitarian thought, he links the Buddhist concept of Nirvana to a "Father" - oriented spirituality, Christianity to a "Son" - oriented spirituality and Advaita in Hinduism to a "Spirit" -oriented spirituality.[50]

1. First Person of the Trinity

The concept of Father is linked to and corresponds to the Absolute, i.e., the transcendent. The Father is encountered in Nirguna Brahman of Hinduism and Nirvana of Buddhism.[51] Panikkar discovers within the spirituality of Buddhism the category of Nirvana to give expression to what he means by the experience of the Father. It is not precisely a phenomenon; it is rather a lack of anything that can be expressed. It is inexpressible, it is *neti neti*, not this, not that. To speak of the Father is to be silent. "Nothing can be said if [*sic*][52] the Father 'in himself,' of the 'self' of the Father. Certainly he is the Father of the Son and Jesus addresses him as Father, but even 'Father' is not his proper name, though he has no other."[53] It is only through the Son and in the Spirit that He is revealed. Nothing can be said of the Father, because he has given up everything through generating the Son. According to Panikkar "The Absolute has no name. All religious traditions have recognized that it is in truth beyond every name . . .,"[54] regardless of the name given within the particular religious system.

In his treatment of the Father, Panikkar applies to the Father all that is beyond the possible names that can be used to describe a reality that is beyond expression. To come to the Father is to move beyond all that can be expressed. Harold Cobb states, "In Panikkar's reformulation the Father is characterized as the Absolute that is beyond every name."[55] Panikkar refers to the Father as "non-Being" and the Source of the Son who is "Being." Everything exists in the Father but is realized in the Son because the Son is the Being of the Father.

Panikkar makes several statements about the Father. First, "the Absolute is One;"[56] secondly, "the Absolute has no name;" thirdly, Christianity has given this Absolute a specific designation, "The Father of our Lord Jesus Christ;"[57] fourthly, plurality or equality attributed to the Three Persons of the Trinity, especially the Father, is inadequate.[58] "Devotion to the Father meets an apophatism of Being; it is a movement towards . . . no place, a prayer which is always open towards . . . the infinite horizon which, like a mirage, always appears in the distance because it is no-where."[59]

For Panikkar devotion to the Father is a movement towards a dimension of self that can be experienced only in terms of silence and that which cannot be expressed. Union with the Father can be experienced only through the Son because "Everything that the Father *is* he transmits to the Son."[60] It is impossible to speak of the Father. Whatever is spoken of the Father is done so in terms of the Word, the Son.[61]

To summarize: For Panikkar the Father is in a realm of the inexpressible. Everything about the Father is expressed through the Son. Panikkar shifts the fulcrum of the theology of the Father from traditional Christian theology to Eastern experiential religious traditions, i.e., the experience of Nirguna Brahman in Hindusim and especially the experience of Nirvana in Buddhism.

2. Second Person of the Trinity

In the work under discussion, *The Trinity and the Religious Experience of Man*, several points surface. First, Panikkar reflects traditional Christian theology in his description of the Second Person of the Trinity. Secondly, he does not remain within the mould of traditional Christian thought. Thirdly, "Christ" has numerous manifestations. Fourthly, every human being can enter into relationship with "Christ" regardless of religion. Still reflecting traditional theology, Panikkar states that it is possible to go to the Father only through the Son:

> It is the Son who acts, who creates. Through him everything was made. In him everything exists. He is the beginning and the end, the alpha and omega. It is the Son, properly speaking - and the Son was manifested in Christ - who is the Divine Person, the Lord.[62]

Panikkar employs tradtional Christian language that is almost identical to the language he used to argue for a place for the concept of Isvara as Christ in his earlier work. Panikkar emphasises that Christ, whether manifest or hidden, remains the only mediator to God the Father.[63] The "unique link between the created and the uncreated, the relative and the absolute, the temporal and the eternal, earth and heaven, is Christ, the only mediator."[64] In *The Unknown Christ of Hinduism* (1964) Panikkar argues for the role of Isvara in the same words: the link between the created and the uncreated, the temporal and the eternal, earth and heaven. Panikkar further suggests that Isvara could be seen as, and indeed is, the hidden Christ in Hinduism.[65]

Although traditional Christian language is used to describe Isvara as the Christ, there is a subtle shift from Christian to Hindu theology in the process. In Hinduism (Advaita), Isvara is Lord. The Lord Isvara is the hidden Christ in Hinduism. This Lord can be called by many names: "I would propose using the word Lord for that Principle, Being, Logos or Christ that other religious traditions call by a variety of names . . ."[66] In this work Panikkar is bolder in his statements regarding the naming of "Christ." Panikkar is also bolder in his statements regarding the relationship between "Christ" and adherents of other religions, even adherents to non-religious traditions. In this work, Panikkar's new concept of "Christ" is the Son with whom all people can enter into personal relationships.

According to Panikkar "it is only with the Son that man can have a personal relationship."[67] It is only with the Son that one can enter into dialogue and communication.[68] "Beings *are* in so far as they participate in the Son, are *from, with and through* him. Every being is a *christophany* a showing forth of Christ."[69]

To summarize: In this work the concept of Christ draws on traditional Christian theology but also moves beyond Christian thought. Christ is present within every religion with expressions and manifestations that move beyond Christian symbols and language. He is known by many names. He is the one with whom every human being can enter into a relationship bringing awareness of the Blessed Trinity.

3. Third Person of the Trinity

In this work, *The Trinity and the Religious Experience of Man*, Panikkar sees the Advaita Vedanta system in Hinduism as the religion that most closely reflects and experiences the Holy Spirit. In keeping with traditional Catholic theology Panikkar maintains the Holy Spirit as the vital link between Father and Son. The Spirit is actively involved as the Father gives everything to the Son. The Spirit is also involved in returning everything that the Father has given to the Son back to the Father.

> The spirit is immanent to Father and Son jointly. In some manner the Spirit 'passes' from Father to Son and from Son to Father in the same process. Just as the Father holds nothing back in his communication of himself to the Son, so the Son does not keep to himself anything that the Father has given him.[70]

Panikkar's trinitarian thought is predicated on the presence of constant motion and activity between the Three Persons of the Trinity. It is the Spirit that allows the Father to "'go on' begetting the Son, because he 'receives back' the very Divinity which he has given up to the Son."[71] The Spirit completes "what Christian theologians used to call the *perichoresis* or *circumincessio*, the dynamic inner circularity of the Trinity."[72]

Panikkar is not satisfied with speaking of the Spirit in terms of the inner life of the Trinity. He moves beyond and equates the Christian concept of the Holy Spirit with the Advaita experience of non-duality. He connects the Christian notion of the Advaita Vedanta notion of the Godhead using the concept of the Holy Spirit as the connecting tissue. In so doing he makes the following connections between Christiantiy and the Advaita system.

First, drawing on the concept of the Spirit, Panikkar shows that the Advaita Vedanta system is a "precious aid in elucidating the intra-trinitarian problem. If the Father and the Son are not *two*, they are not one either: the Spirit both unites and distinguishes them."[73]

Secondly, Panikkar points out that the Spirit, as recognized within the Advaita Vedanta system, emables one to speak adequately about the Godhead in relationship with human beings: "Indeed what is the Spirit but the *atman* of the Upanisads, which is said to be identical with *brahman*, although this identity can only be existentially recognized and affirmed once 'realization' has been attained?" [74] Panikkar insists, not only that "one finds that at the deepest level of the Divinity what there is is the Spirit,"[75] but also that what one finds at thc deepest level of the human person is the Atman, the Spirit.

Panikkar appeals further to Eastern thought to elaborate on the relationship of the Spirit with the individual:

> He who knows that *brahman* exists - his is an indirect knowledge; he who knows: 'I am *brahman*' - his is a direct knowledge'. 'I am *brahman*' in so far as it is not *brahman* who says so. The one who can speak thus does it only as the Spirit and the Word who is thus spoken is the Logos.[76]

Thirdly, Panikkar describes the role of the Spirit in the area of prayer as it relates to the Advaita Vedanta system.

> One cannot pray *to* the Spirit as an isolated term of our prayer. One can only have a non-relational union with him. One can only pray *in* the Spirit, by addressing the Father through the Son. It is rather the Spirit, who prays in us.[77]

Panikkar's claim that one cannot pray to the Spirit as an isolated term of our prayer and that one can have only a non-relational union with the Spirit is moving dramatically closer to the Hindu concept of the Godhead.

Fourthly, Panikkar sometimes refers to the Spirit as "Return of Being (or the ocean of Being)."[78] Panikkar understands the "return of Being" to be the "end of Being."[79] It is the Spirit that enables human beings to exist and evolve into "full" or "Self-Realized" human beings.

Fifthly, Panikkar explains the necessity of the Spirit for achieving divinization: "So long as the Spirit has not been received, it is impossible to understand the message brought by the Son and, equally, to reach *theosis*, the divinization that the Spirit realizes in man."[80] Here we have a dramatic instance of bridge-building between the role of the Spirit in the Christian concept of the Trinity and the Hindu statement, that divinization is realized in the individual.

To summarize: In this work Panikkar draws on traditional Christian Pneumatology as well as on Hinduism (Advaita) in the development of his thought regarding the Holy Spirit. Panikkar envisions the experience of the Holy Spirit as most evident in the Advaita tradition of Hinduism. The Spirit returns to the Father all that is given to the Son. Also, the Spirit grounds the non-dualistic experience of Atman (innermost Self) equaling Brahman (God) and the divinization process realized within the individual.

C. Other Works

There are two works of Panikkar from the early and mid 1970's which, while not bearing directly on the Trinity, deal with strands of his thought that will have implications for his later trinitarian formulation: "Have 'Religions' the Monopoly on *Religion*?"[81] and "The Contribution of Christian Monasticism in Asia to the Universal Church."[82] These articles are especially representative of some of the connective tissue that coalesces into a unified whole in Panikkar's later trinitarian concept. What is significant about these writings is that they represent the stirrings taking place in his thought, which will later result in radically new trinitarian emphases.

The first article, written in 1974, is entitled "Have 'Religions' the Monopoly on *Religion*?" Panikkar's answer to the question is a resounding "No!" Traditional "religions" are *ways* to salvation, which is defined as "anything making one whole, healthy, free, and complete."[83] However, the same struggle for human fullness is being promoted by human enterprises that are not "religious" in the strict sense: ideologies, humanisms, and even atheisms.[84] Panikkar concludes the article with a vigorous plea for encounter and dialogue between all human enterprises, whether named religions, ideologies, humanisms, atheisms, or the like, "which pretend to 'better' the present human condition . . ."[85]   Only then, he adds, "we could perhaps discover one of the fundamental and enduring tasks of all *religion*: the rescue of humanity from the danger of perishing."[86]

There are two elements in this article pertinent to Panikkar's later trinitarian thought. First, the dynamics are already at work to de-emphasize the structures of organized religions. Panikkar did not want to dismantle religious structures; however, he saw that they could also be obstacles to the discovery and experience of the Blessed Trinity in all its depth and universality.

Secondly, salvation is equated with human "wholeness," understood in a naturalistic sense. The earlier Panikkar reflects traditional Christian trinitarian doctrine: the Trinity has saved and continues to save all of humanity. However, as his thought progresses, the Trinity becomes more and more the source of salvation, i.e., wholeness, even outside of the structures of organized religion. The earlier Panikkar is not explicit in stating the relationship between "wholeness" and the Trinity. However, the seeds are already planted in the thought of the earlier Panikkar that will eventually flower in his later trinitarian thought.

The second article of Panikkar to be examined in this section is "The Contribution of Christian Monasticism in Asia to the Universal Church" and, in particular, the subsection entitled, "The Threefold Mystery." He calls this subsection, "a reflection on a monastic theology of history."

Panikkar states that "the threefold mystery of reality" is the universal reality that is described in various ways, such as in the "Bhagavad Gita, St. Paul and many other sacred texts."[87]   In the article, as in some of his earlier writings, Panikkar starts making a clearer distinction between the traditional Christian concept of the Trinity and his own development of what he claims to be a truly universal trinitarian vision. The subsection of the article, "The Threefold Mystery," begins by formulating "the mystery" in Christian terms. First, there is the mystery of *"Creation*, the work of the Father, the unfathomable Source and groundless ground of all that is."[88]   Secondly, there is the mystery of *"Incarnation*, the action of the Son, the field of history, the place of the Logos."[89]   Thirdly, there is the mystery of *"Glorification*, the mission of the Spirit, the sacred struggling action wherein man and cosmos are transfigured, the process of enlightenment, the divinization of all that has come out of God."[90]

In this very brief text, Panikkar appeals to Africa, the Western world and Asia as typifying awareness of the Threefold Mystery, respectively, as Creation, Incarnation and Glorification. Yet, he is careful not to exaggerate the comparisions. He states, "We should not oversimplify or compartmentalize, we should avoid neat theories."[91]

What arises in this text is a new orientation of Panikkar's trinitarian thought. In pointing to Africa as best describing "The mystery of *Creation*, the work of the Father, . . . this first moment of the mystery of reality," Panikkar asserts, "Is it not the genius of Africa . . . to be sensitive to all the values of creation, to the transcendentally indwelling Origin which makes words and any other expression secondary?"[92]

This article's treatment of the Father presents three instances of inconsistency when compared with other works of the earlier Panikkar. First, it is most unusual for Panikkar to connect the "Father" with "creation." In the other works of the earlier Panikkar, the Father is still Origin or Source and is associated with silence and lack of expression, but not with creation. In his other works Panikkar associates "the second moment of the mystery of reality" with creation. It is Christ who is Creator.[93]

The second unusual facet of this article is the attribution of indwelling to the Father. When the earlier Panikkar refers to indwelling in his other works, he is speaking of the Trinity as Three Persons, or of "Christ" in the universal sense that Panikkar applies to him, or of the Spirit that dwells within.[94]

The third unusual aspect of his article is the treatment of the "silence" of the Father: ". . . the transcendentally indwelling Origin . . . makes words and any other expression secondary."[95] In his other earlier works Panikkar nuances this statement considerably. The Father's silence and lack of expression are absolute. "Words and other expression" are not only "secondary" but altogether nonexistent.[96]

In relation to the second moment of the mystery of reality, that is, "the mystery of Incarnation," Panikkar's article speaks of the achievement of the West in terms of discovering "the unique value of history, the world-transforming power of the logos, the place of the Incarnation."[97] He associates the West with what is Jewish, Christian and Islamic[98] : in effect, cultures which elsewhere he depicts as emphasizing personalism and loving devotion to the Godhead.[99] Although Panikkar gives this rare praise to the achievement of the West in relation to the Godhead, in the same article he states "the era of God is waning."[100] He is not denying here that God is alive. "Certainly . . . God is alive, but in a deeper and transformed sense."[101]

This deepening and transformation, according to Panikkar, will come about only through a gradual reinterpretation of the Christian Trinity against the horizon of the Asian[102] tradition.

In the article Panikkar goes on to categorize the third moment of the mystery of reality as best expressed by Asians: "the mystery of *Glorification*, the mission of this Spirit."[103] Panikkar is rethinking the Christian Trinity against the backdrop of the Advaita tradition and is appealing to the depth-experience and self-realization[104] of the Advaitin as the depth-experience of the Trinity, although in the context he is referring explicitly to the Christian monastic tradition in Asia.

He states that the "apophatic dimension of the real is what best characterizes the Asian soul." The experience of this dimension is found within the "field of the Spirit, the experience of realization, the ever-present presence of the *eschaton*, not in terms of *eschatology* but in epiphany."[105] Here Panikkar is appealing especially to Asian Catholics to bring about the awareness and depths of meaning that are waiting to be discovered in the Threefold Mystery, that is, the Trinity. He states that the ". . .time is ripening for this really universal and catholic cooperation."[106] The Asian vocation is one of "sensitizing the world, 'conscientizing' man to his transcendent, vertical reality."[107]

D. Summary

Panikkar's earlier thought exemplifies a movement towards an understanding of the Trinity that encompasses the universal experience of humanity, both individually and collectively. In *The Unknown Christ of Hinduism* (1964) he speaks a language of faith in the person of Christ, in whom he sees the entire expression of God the Father. In *The Trinity and the Religious Experience of Man* (1973) he views the Trinity against the horizon of the religious experience of the world community, especially Buddhism (Father), Christianity (Son) and Hinduism (Holy Spirit). In the earlier Panikkar, there are several aspects of his thought that are noteworthy.

First, even though Panikkar is working with a somewhat traditional concept of the Trinity, he has difficulty seeing the Father and Spirit as Persons.[108]

In Panikkar's theology it is only in Christ in the wider sense that the revelation of God has been unveiled as person. It is only in the very early Panikkar (1964) that one finds a clear statement that the revelation of God has been fully revealed in Jesus Christ. The early Panikkar is well aware of the other "Christs" as being problematic in terms of Person. In Panikkar's early thought there is a tendency to play down personalism in religion. "Religious personalism is after all only a purification of idolatry."[109]

Secondly, his contact with the East provides the categories for critiquing traditional trinitarian teachings, or more accurately, for formulating new ways of thinking about the Trinity.[110] In so doing he rethinks Christian, Hindu and Buddhist doctrines. The Father (Nirvana) is the absolute, the transcendent, the inexpressible; Christ (Jesus, Isvara, Buddha, etc.) is the being in whom expression of the Father is given; the Spirit (Advaita) is that which completes the trinitarian cycle within the depths of the human person.

Thirdly, in these earlier works of Panikkar there is a definitive progression of thought. His major problem is the historical Jesus. He combs the Christian Scriptures in order to add credibility to his thought.[111] In the 1960's the fullness of revelation in Jesus dominates his trinitarian thought. In the 1970's, he is still convinced of the fullness of revelation in Jesus, but not with the same intensity as in the previous decade. In the mid 1970's that aspect of his thought breaks down rapidly. He is no longer concerned with the traditional issues of the Sacraments and the Holy Spirit dwelling in the Church. He now functions with new perspectives and is driven by a new awareness of the authentic experience of God in the world religions. He pursues the question of Jesus more radically.[112] His concern is to face the problem directly; to rethink the question of Jesus as Saviour of the world; to present the historical Jesus within the category of the Logos, but in the light of the world religions; to assimilate the experience of "Christ" within the system of the Advaita Vedanta tradition, not only on the level of concepts and theories, but also through a direct connection with the experience of the Advaitin (Atman equals Brahman). To do this Panikkar has had to equate Isvara with "Christ." Although the earlier Panikkar becomes gradually more immersed in the Eastern systems, his categories can still be reconciled with traditional Christian thought.

Fourthly, in the 1960's there appears in Panikkar a tendency to present the Triune God of Christianity in a language that is credible to Hindus as well as to those of other religions. His trinitarian thought in the 1970's is less traditional. He is now speaking primarily to a Christian audience and arguing for a revision of some of the traditional beliefs regarding Christology and the Trinity.

Fifthly, Panikkar holds that nothing can be predicated of the Father, because He has no "relations" with human beings except through "Christ".[114] "Christ" becomes a universal category with numerous manifestations. The Spirit is spoken of, but in a new sense. In keeping with traditional Christian theology, Panikkar speaks of the Spirit as completing the cycle within the Triune God. However, Panikkar moves beyond traditional trinitarian thought by expanding the role of the Spirit within the Advaita Vedanta tradition of Hinduism. The Spirit enables the Advaitin's awareness of the Godhead to take place, completing what Panikkar recognizes to be a trinitarian experience, where Atman equals Brahman, that is, the Innermost Self equals God.

Sixthly, the earlier Panikkar is aware of the problems that emerge from the Western emphasis on time and history. It is this emphasis that is responsible for the Christian adhering tightly to Jesus Christ as the exclusive fullness of God's revelation, resulting in the suppression of true universality in religious thought. The religious schools with which the earlier Panikkar is dialoguing, namely Advaita Vedanta and Buddhism, have little use for time and history in their understanding of "God's" revelation. This does not mean that time and history are not highly regarded. It is their way of thinking about "God" (or the non-expressible God) that breaks through time and history and even space.[115]

Seventhly, from Panikkar's emphasis on "Christ" with the many expressions in the various religious traditions,[116] it might appear that he abandons the traditional theory that God is fully revealed in Jesus Christ. In fact, he never negates it, he never abandons it. What the earlier Panikkar does is become increasingly silent about the topic.

Eighthly, there is a tendency within the period of the earlier Panikkar to view the Trinity as functioning within the human person. The Triune God emerges from the "within" experience of the individual where one goes "beyond" one's highest Self to be encompassed by a trinitarian experience that is also a fully human experience. In the earlier Panikkar there are traces of the "incarnation" of the Triune God within human persons. It is a valid question to ask whether the earlier Panikkar deemphasizes Jesus or elevates human persons to the level of God. He does neither; however, one can be left with such questions.

In conclusion, Panikkar's earlier writings expressing his trinitarian thought are not always clear. The two traditions of Christianity and Hinduism that he is trying to harmonize under the umbrella of the Trinity do not always connect. In fact, he reinterprets both traditions. He has some difficulty in moving from a Christ-centered concept of Trinity to what he considers a more integrated concept. Trinity as seen from its universal horizon (Christianity, Hinduism and Buddhism) and Trinity as seen within the Advaitin experience never quite meet in the writings of the early Panikkar. His earlier trinitarian thought, undergoing many twists and turns, still remains ambiguous.

Notes

1 For example, the Preface to Panikkar's text *Trinity and Religious Experience* was written at Easter of 1973. He stated in the Preface, "This study was written ten years ago in Uttarikashi in the heart of the Himalayas in a small hut on the shore of the Ganges." Panikkar, *Trinity and Religious Experience*, vii.

2 The first Foreword to this text was written on Easter of 1957, indicating that most of the book has been written prior to 1957. Five years later the second Foreword was written on Easter of 1962 with indications that further changes had been made in the text. The next principal early text, *The Trinity and the Religious Experience of Man* (1973), was first partially published in German under the title *Kerygma und Indien. Zur heilsgeschichtlichen Problematik der christlichen Begegnung mit Indien* (Hamburg: Herbert Reich, 1967). It was later published with slight revisions in English under several different titles.

3 Panikkar, *Unknown Christ of Hinduism* (1964), 26.

4 *Ibid.*

5 See *ibid.*, 119-131.

6 *Ibid.*, 119.

7 Nikhilananda, *The Upanishads*, 164.

8 For Panikkar, this is not just an Indian question. "This is in my opinion not just a Vedantic problem; in the final analysis, the *amr* of the Koran, the *Logos* of Plotinus and the *Tathagata* of Buddhism, for example, spring from a similar view as to the necessity for an ontological link between these two apparently irreconcilable poles: the absolute and the relative." Panikkar, *Unknown Christ of Hinduism* (1964), 120.

9 *Ibid.*

10 *Ibid.*, 126. See also 128.

11 See *ibid.*, 138.

12 "Christ does not belong to Christianity, he only belongs to God," *ibid.*, 20.

13 "Christ does not belong to Christianity, he belongs to his Father only," *ibid.* (1981), 54.

14 *Ibid.* (1964), 124.

15 *Ibid.* (1964), 126. Admittedly Panikkar is lacking in precision when he makes a distinction between God the Father, as "the source of the whole Divinity" and the Son, as "that from which all things proceed and to which all things return."

16 Panikkar, *Unknown Christ of Hinduism* (1964), 126.

17 See "Advaita and Trinity," *ibid.*, 119 - 131.

18 See *ibid.*, 124.

19 See *ibid.*

20 *Ibid.*, 125.

21 Not in the sense that Saguna Brahman is lesser them Nirguna Brahman, as in Advaitin thought expressed by philosophers such as Sankara, but more in the sense of equality with different faces.

22 Maya is considered illusion or unreality. Maya is also responsible for the material cause of the universe, which results in Appearance. Brahman, which is attributeless, when linked with maya "becomes" or appears to be endowed with the attributes of creation, preservation and destruction. The whole creation is maya, a "power belonging to the Lord Himself and hidden in its own gunas." (Svetasvatara Upanishad I.3).

23 This is one instance where Panikkar changes Hindu (Advaitin) doctrine.

24 Panikkar, *Unknown Christ of Hinduism* (1964), 126 - 127.

25 Isvara is present also in other Hindu systems of thought. See Swami Prabhavananda, *The Spiritual Heritage of India* (Hollywood: Vedanta Press, 1963), 227-28, 231, 288-92, 304. See also Nikhilananda, *The Upanishads*, 44-5, 127, 128. Panikkar uses the term Isvara taking into account its development in Hindu thought.

26 See Panikkar, *Unknown Christ of Hinduism* (1964), 122 -124.

27 *Ibid.*, 122.

28 See *ibid.*

29 See *ibid.*, 123.

30 See *ibid.*

31 See *ibid.*, 123 - 124; See the following Hindu texts in order to grasp the meaning of the Hindu concept of incarnation (avatar meaning "going through"): *Mahabharat*, 12.59.5, 13-30, 93-94; *Visnu Purana*, 1.22.84; *Skanda Purana, Suta Samhita*, 4.2.3.114-16; Sharngadeva's Sangitratnakara, 1.3.1-2, 13; *Bhagavad Gita*, 10.20-24, 40-42; 11.3-4, 8. 14-17, 21, 26-27, 31-34; 9.22-34; 18.66-69; *Bhagavata Purana*, 3.29.7-34; 6.1.11-18; 6.2.14; 7.5.24; 11.3.18-32; 11.27.7-51; Lakacharya's *Tattvatraya*, 85 ff., 121 ff. See also Immanuel Rajappan, *The Influence of Hinduism on Indian Christians* (Jabalpur: Leonard Theological College, 1950), 17-85; G. Parrinder, *Avatar and Incarnation* (New York: Barnes and Noble, 1970); Joseph Mattam, "Dialogue and Incarnation," *Land of the Trinity* (Bangalore: Theological Publications in India, 1975), 95-96.

32 See Panikkar, *Unknown Christ of Hinduism* (1964), 124.

33 *Ibid.*, 131.

34 *Ibid.*

35 *Ibid.*, 21.

36 *Ibid.*, ix.

37 Revised Foreword for *Unknown Christ of Hinduism* (1964), xii.

38 *Ibid.*, xi.

39 *Ibid.*, x.

40 *Ibid.*, xi.

41 See *ibid.*, 26.

42 *Ibid.*, 131.

43 *Ibid.*, viii.

44 *Ibid.*, xii.

45 *Ibid.*, 26.

46 *Ibid.*, 60.

47 *Ibid.*, 6.

48 *Ibid.*, 26.

49 This section, as indeed most of the book, i.e., Chapter II and III, constitute his doctoral dissertation in theology, defended at the very traditional Lateran University of Rome in 1961.

50 See Panikkar, *Trinity and Religious Experience*, 41-69.

51 For a general Hindu concept of God and its relation to Brahman see Jitendra N. Banerjea, in "The Hindu Concept of God," *The Religion of the Hindus*, ed. Kenneth Morgan (New York: Ronald Press, 1953), 48-82. For an elaboration of the concept of Nirvana see Raimundo Panikkar "Nirvana and the Awareness of the Absolute," *The God Experience*, ed. Joseph Whelan (New York: Newman Press, 1971), 81-99.

52 Obvious typographical error for "of."

53 Panikkar, *Trinity and Religious Experience*, 46.

54 *Ibid.*, 44.

55 Harold Coward, *Pluralism: Challenge to World Religions* (Maryknoll: Orbis Books, 1985), 43.

56 Panikkar, *Trinity and Religious Experience*, 44.

57 *Ibid.*

58 See *ibid.*

59 *Ibid.*, 48.

60 *Ibid.*, 46.

61 See *ibid.*, 47.

62 *Ibid.*, 51.

63 See *ibid.*, 53.

64 *Ibid.*

65 See Panikkar, *Unknown Chirst of Hinduism* (1964), 119-131.

66 Panikkar, *Trinity and Religious Experience*, 53.

67 *Ibid.*, 52.

68 See *ibid.*

69 *Ibid.*, 54.

70 *Ibid.*, 60.

71 *Ibid.*

72 *Ibid.*

73 *Ibid.*, 62.

74 *Ibid.*, 63-64.

75 *Ibid.*, 60.

76 *Ibid.*, 64.

77 *Ibid.*, 63.

78   Raymond Panikkar, "Toward an Ecumenical Theandric Spirituality," *Journal of Ecumenical Studies* 5 (1968): 533. See also the identical words in Panikkar, *Trinity and World Religions*, 67.

79   Panikkar, *Trinity and World Religions*, 67.

80   *Ibid.*

81   Raimundo Panikkar, "Have 'Religions' the Monopoly on Religion?", *Journal of Ecumenical Studies* 11 (1974): 515-517.

82   Raymond Panikkar, "The Contribution of Christian Monasticism in Asia to the Universal Church," *Cistercian Studies* 10 (1975): 73-84. The article is the closing address which Panikkar gave to the second Asian Monastic Congress in Bangalore October, 1973.

83   Panikkar, "Have 'Religions' the Monopoly on Religion?", 515.

84   See *ibid.*, 516.

85   *Ibid.*, 517.

86   *Ibid.*

87   Panikkar, "The Contribution of Christian Monasticism," 81.

88   *Ibid.*

89   *Ibid.*

90   *Ibid.*

91   *Ibid.*

92   *Ibid.*

93   See Panikkar, *Unknown Christ of Hinduism* (1964), 126.

94   See *ibid.*, ix, xii, 17.

95   Panikkar, "The Contribution of Christian Monasticism," 81.

96   See Panikkar, "Toward an Ecumenical Theandric Spirituality," 522-526.

97   Panikkar, "The Contribution of Christian Monasticism," 81.

98   See *ibid.*

99   See Panikkar, *Trinity and Religious Experience*, 51-58.

101 Panikkar, "The Contribution of Christian Monasticism," 82.

102 Panikkar in reality excludes the Bhakti tradition. Actually he is referring only to the Advaita and similar Eastern traditions.

103 Panikkar, "The Contribution of Christian Monasticism," 82.

104 Self-realization is achieved when Atman (Innermost Self) equals Brahman (God), when the Innermost Self is intimately in union with the Divine (non-duality).

105 Panikkar, "The Contribution of Christian Monasticism," 81.

106 *Ibid.*

107 *Ibid.*

108 See Panikkar, *Trinity and World Religions*, 45-50 and 57-67.

109 Panikkar, "Toward an Ecumenical Theandric Spirituality," 514.

110 See ibid., 509 - 522.

111 In many of his articles and books, Panikkar cites numerous examples from the Bible, especially the Letters of Paul and the Gospels (in particular, the Gospel of John). For example, see Panikkar, *Unknown Christ of Hinduism* (1964), 127.

112 See Raimundo Panikkar, "The Meaning of Christ's Name in the Universal Economy of Salvation," in *Evangelization, Dialogue and Development*, ed. Mariasusai Dhavamony (Rome: Università Gregoriana Editrice, 1972), 195-218. See also a slightly revised version: *Salvation in Christ: Concreteness and Universality, the Supername* (Santa Barbara: privately published, 1972), 16-45.

114 "Christ" is used here in Panikkar's sense of the Logos.

115 See Nikhilananda, *The Upanishads*, 164-167. See also verses 1 and 3.

116 "This Christ present, active, unknown and hidden may be called Isvara, Bhagavan, or even 'Krishna,' 'Narayana' or 'Siva.'" Raymond Panikkar, "Confrontation between Hinduism and Christ," *New Blackfriars* 50 (1969): 203.

Chapter III

The Later Panikkar
on Trinity (1981-93)

Panikkar's later thinking on the Trinity emerges as a development of his earlier thought as seen in Chapter II. His later understanding, although not radically new, moves forward substantially from his earlier thought on the Trinity.

Section A of this chapter will examine Panikkar's later trinitarian thought from the second edition of his *The Unknown Christ of Hindusim* (1981). Section B will treat some trinitarian themes in the light of an article, "The Jordan, the Tiber, and the Ganges" (1987). Section C will summarize Lecture Six, "The Radical Trinity," of the Gifford Lectures (1989). Although this lecture is unpublished, it reflects aspects of Panikkar's trinitarian theology not found elsewhere and therefore not to be overlooked. Section D will pursue Panikkar's thought in the Warren Lecture given at the University of Tulsa in 1991. Although this lecture does not deal directly with Panikkar's theology of Trinity, it clearly evidences insights of his more current trinitarian thought. Aspects of the Bellarmine Lecture given by Panikkar in 1991 will be treated in Section E. This lecture deals primarily with Panikkar's Christology, with strands of trinitarian theology. The final section of this chapter, section F, will briefly summarize Panikkar's later trinitarian thought.

A. *Second Edition of* The Unknown
Christ of Hinduism (1981)

This section of the chapter will simply state Panikkar's trinitarian theology as indicated in the work, with special emphasis on areas where the 1981 edition differs from the 1964 edition. The development of his trinitarian thought from the 1964 to the 1981 edition will be addressed in Chapter IV.

In his *The Unknown Christ of Hindusim* (1981) Panikkar attempts to remain faithful to his 1964 text in order to be consistent with it original intent. At the same time he tries to be equally faithful to his new way of thinking about the Triune God. The result is twofold. On the one hand, he changes the text only slightly in order to retain the original thought. On the other hand, he inserts entire paragraphs or pages to express his more recent understanding. These additions are more often trinitarian rather than christological. As a result, in this edition Panikkar's trinitarian thought is presented with greater clarity. The Trinity in this work is still expressed in two ways: either "Father, Logos and Holy Spirit"[2] or "Father, Christ and Holy Spirit."[3]

In addition, Panikkar equates all reality with the Trinity: "All that exists, i.e., the whole of reality is nothing but God: Father, Christ and Holy Spirit."[4] This last way of linking all of reality with the Trinity is almost identical to Advaitin thought about the Godhead.

1. Saccidananda

Panikkar introduces the Hindu concept of Saccidananda in his 1981 edition of *The Unknown Christ of Hindusim.* Saccidananda has been often used by both Christian and Hindu scholars when making comparisons between the Trinity and "similar" concepts within Hinduism.[5] The term Saccidananda is a composite of three words: Sat (Reality, Existence, Being or Truth); Cit (Consciousness or Knowledge); and Ananda (Bliss, Joy or Happiness).[6]

Saccidananda as a symbol of Brahman described the perception of Brahman by the Advaitin. The basis of knowing Brahman lies not in speculation or reason, but in the experience of Brahman by Advaitins.

Panikkar refers to the term Saccidananda three times in this 1981 edition. First, he explains its meaning. Panikkar describes Sat (Reality) as the "support of all that in one way or another constitutes being."[7] Cit (Consciousness) is the "spiritual or intellectual link that encompasses and penetrates the total reality."[8] Ananda (Bliss) is the "perfect fullness that receives into itself and inspires all that is tending towards it."[9]

Secondly, Panikkar uses the concept of Saccidananda as further basis for showing how the Second Person of the Trinity is needed to supply the relational aspect of God. Panikkar presents this relational aspect in terms of the many manifestations of the Hindu God(s). He states that there is a tendency for the religious person to want to bow to the Ultimate. In a sense, "the Hindu may bow to the ultimacy of *Saccidananda Brahman*, while in his need for the concrete he acknowledges that Siva (or Krishna or Kali) is the be-all[10] and end-all of the universe . . ."[11]

Thirdly, Panikkar refers to this same concept when describing the need for Isvara. He states "Brahman is often said to be pure being, consciousness and bliss: *sat, cit and ananda*."[12] Because this concept of God is "devoid of relations,"[13] Isvara is needed to provide the relational sense: "Isvara is existence, consciousness and bliss in the relational sense."[14]

Panikkar does not explicitly connect Saccidananda with the Christian notion of Trinity; however, he does use the concept of Saccidananda to assist him in the development of his understanding of the Second Person of the Trinity in the context of the many manifestations of the Hindu Gods.

2. First Person of the Trinity

God is essentially: ". . . Brahman, . . . or the Divinity as Absolute, without relation, immutable, unique, simple."[15] Here God is not differentiated in terms of Father, Son and Holy Spirit. Yet what Panikkar is actually referring to is the Father. It is the Father who is the Source of life. Life flows out of the Father alone, as source. The Father pours forth everything into the Son. The Father is expressed only through the Son. Panikkar states, "In him [i.e., Christ] all things are summed up and the Spirit will quicken them with that life which flows out of the Father alone."[16] Panikkar's treatment of the First Person of the Trinity remains basically the same in both the 1964 and 1981 editions of *The Unknown Christ of Hindusim*.

3. Second Person of the Trinity

In this work, as in the earlier edition, "Christ," i.e., the Logos, God the Son, is Isvara.[17] It is Christ "who inspires the prayers of Man and makes them 'audible' to the Father."[18] Christ is the universal saviour.[19] Christ "does not belong to Christianity; he belongs to his Father only."[20] According to Panikkar "Christ is already present in Hinduism. The Spirit of Christ is already at work in Hindu prayer."[21] The presence of Christ is in no way less than in Christianity.

What is added in this new edition is the observation that Isvara is "the Christ" of Hinduism, and not (as presented in the 1964 edition) just the "Hidden" or "Unknown" Christ of Hinduism in the Advaita Vedanta tradition.[22]   More importantly in this new edition Panikkar deletes the expression "the Logos became man . . ."[23] in favor of "the Logos is Man . . ." Panikkar declares in his new edition: "And faith in turn allows me to enter into the ineffable heart of Divinity, there to discover, to understand that this Father is omnipotent, creator, and that the Logos is Man . . ."[24] Panikkar is not referring here specifically to Jesus or to any of the Gods of the other religious traditions. He is referring to the enlightened human being in oneness with God, that is Atman equals Brahman.

4. Third Person of the Trinity

The most striking change regarding the Holy Spirit in this new edition is the following. "(T)he Spirit is the living breath of his People and of the universe"[25] replaces the wording of the 1964 edition: "the Spirit breathes on his Church."[26] The focus and scope of the Spirit is broadened from the Roman Catholic Church to God's People in general and to the very universe.

A second instance of a change concerning the Holy Spirit in the two editions is the following. In the 1964 edition the encounter between Christianity and Hindusim is described as taking place "because it is an encounter in Christ already present in the heart of the two *bona fide* partners."[27] In the 1981 edition he writes: "We are referring to the Spirit of God as the place where the encounter, if at all, takes place. It is only in the Holy Spirit that prayers meet, intentions coalesce and persons enter into communion."[28] Therefore, in the new edition there is a shift in emphasis from Christ to the Holy Spirit as the point of encounter between Christians and Hindus.

A third change in the way Panikkar treats of the Holy Spirit in the two editions of the work under consideration is the expression itself. In the 1964 edition the terminology for the Third Person of the Trinity is very traditional. In the 1981 edition Panikkar states that what " . . . Christians will consider the Holy Spirit or the Spirit of Christ"[29] can be referred to by Hindus as "the Spirit of God . . . which the Hindus will interpret as the Divine *Sakti*[30] penetrating everything and manifesting God, disclosing him in his immanence and being present in all his manifestations . . ."[31] Therefore, in this new edition the Holy Spirit is expressed in a wider variety of terms.

In his attempt to link the Hindu (Advaita) and the Christian concepts of the Godhead, Panikkar in this new edition further emphasizes the need for the individual, religious or not, to experience and come to terms with the cosmotheandric realtiy.[32]   In the 1964 edition Panikkar asserts: "Christianity is the fullness of religion and thus the real per-fection of every religion."[33]   In the 1981 edition he speaks of the lack of "fullness" in any religious system:

> But the only way that Hinduism will become fuller is to be composed principally of people who have mystically realized that fullness of Man. Christianity itself is not statistically any "fuller" in this respect. The same is therefore, true of it: it must become "filled" with people who have experienced the cosmotheandric reality.[34]

Although stated in a subtle way, the "fullness of Man" is equated with the "fullness of God that can be realized."[35]   The cosmotheandric mystery can be expressed under many names, including "Krishna or Justice or Woman."[36]

B. "The Jordan, the Tiber, and the Ganges. Three Kairological Moments of Christic Self Consciousness" (1987)

This article deals with the question of what it means today to be a Christian. Panikkar examines this question through the perspective of the history of Christian tradition in its relation to other religions as symbolized by the three rivers, i.e., the Jordan, the Tiber and the Ganges. Reflecting on religious pluralism Panikkar arrives at a "quasi" treatment of the Trinity. His treatment, though not explicitly related to trinitarian theology, is useful in providing some insights into his later trinitarian thought. What follows will be summary statements relevant to Trinity, extracted from the article.

First, Panikkar depicts the Trinity as the "ultimate foundation for pluralism."[38] This pluralism, however, reflects a "nondualistic, advaitic attitude, that defends the pluralism of truth because reality itself is pluralistic."[39] The following excerpt sheds light on Panikkar's "revised" concept of the Trinity:

Being as such, even if "encompassed" by or "co-existent" with the Logos or a Supreme Intelligence, does not need to be reduced to consciousness. The perfect self-mirroring of Being is truth, but even if the perfect image of Being is identical to Being, Being is not exhausted in its image. If the Logos is the transparency of Being, the Spirit is, paradoxically, its opaqueness. The Spirit is freedom, the freedom of Being to be what it is. And this is, *a priori* as it were, unforeseeable by the Logos. The Logos accompanies Being; it does not precede it; it does not predict what Being is. But the *is* of Being is free.[40]

This statement by Panikkar treats the Logos and the Spirit in terms of Being. Here Panikkar again speaks of a trinitarian concept that is clearly universal and "pluralistic" because its fulcrum centres on Being. However, it also eludes religious constructs because it is rooted in the concept of Being. Although Panikkar claims that the Trinity is the "ultimate foundation of pluralism," this pluralism is not seen within the context of different world religions, but rather in terms of "reality" that is "pluralistic." For Panikkar, the Trinity that is the ultimate foundation for pluralism, is seen against the horizon of non-dualism, that is Advaita.[41]

The second statement that directly bears on Panikkar's trinitarian thought is again related to pluralism. Pluralism "expresses an attitude of cosmic confidence (in the Spirit, which is not subordinate to the Logos)."[42] Panikkar claims that this "allows for a polar and tensile co-existence between *ultimate* human attitudes, cosmologies, and religions."[43]

The Spirit and the Logos are again presented in a context of universality that moves outside the "confines" of religion and is grounded within the human person.

The third and final statement bears directly on Panikkar's revised treatment of the Second Person of the Trinity. Panikkar affirms:

The Christian pluralist will not affirm that there are many saviors. This is a nonpluralistic assertion. The pluralistic christological affirmation will begin - as with the Trinity (*Qui incipit numerare incipit errare* ["who begins to count, begins to err"] said Augustine) - by denying the meaningfulness of any quantitative individualization in the Mystery of Christ. The saving power - which Christians call Christ - is neither one nor many.[44]

What is significant in this text is Panikkar's treatment of the concept of "many saviours" and "pluralism." It appears as if he is moving from his previous insistence on the concept of many "Christs," i.e., "many saviours" or "many manifestations of the Logos" to a concept of "Christ" that is now "not one nor many."

Panikkar makes several other statements that are significant for his trinitarian thought, although they do not bear directly on the Trinity. First, exegetical approaches are inadequate. Secondly, revelation from other sacred books is vital to Christian awareness. Thirdly, salvation needs to be seen within the context of the Ganges, the symbol of the East. Fourthly, Panikkar claims that having a single view of Christ is inadequate even if this view is broadly conceived. Fifthly, "each religion may be a dimension of the other in a kind of trinitarian *perichoresis* or *circumincessio*."[45]   Sixthly, Panikkar insists that if "Christians are able to extricate from their own religion the christic principle, this principle can be experienced as a dimension at least potentially present in any human being, as long as no absolute interpretation is given."[46]   However, he also qualifies this statement with the claim that this can also be said of similar principles in other traditions such as Buddhahood in Buddhism. Seventhly, Panikkar presents his concept of "christic principle" as the "point of union, understanding, and love with all humankind and with the whole of the cosmos."[47]   He further states that a deep awareness of the "christic principle" requires transcending "religious constructs."[48]

C. Gifford Lecture Six: *"The Radical Trinity" (1989)*

Although as yet unpublished, these lectures are being considered in this study because Panikkar values them as a very important expression of his current thinking.[49]   Of the ten lectures, the one that is most relevant is Lecture Six, "The Radical Trinity," delivered on May 4, 1989.

In this lecture, Panikkar seeks to deepen and broaden Christian trinitarian understanding. He states that the Trinity needs to be seen with a valid universal methodic.[50]   He goes beyond both the immanent and economic Trinity of Christian theology, because he claims that in both cases the Trinity seems to be the privilege of a separate Godhead. Panikkar introduces the notion of "radical Trinity" to show that the trinitarian intuition is the most fundamental characteristic of reality. Being itself is trinitarian. In elucidating Trinity he probes the collective experience of the human memory, which includes the history of many cultures, not just of Christianity.

Panikkar's mature treatment of the Trinity moves far beyond his earlier thought on the subject, although cosmotheandrism is still central. The sources of his mature thought are somewhat different. He draws on anthropology, science, mathematics, philosophy and religion, as well as the contemporary consciousness of the human person and the current global situation.

Panikkar begins his treatment of the Trinity by recalling the universal "threeness" that is found in the history of religions and in many other traditions and cultures. He refers to the Trikaya Buddha and Saccidananda[51] as well as several other examples. He makes reference also to the *vestigia Trinitatis* present in non-christian religions; however, he holds that the *vestigia Trinitatis* theory flows from presuppositions that are not necessary.

Philosophically, threeness is an essential dimension of the mind; but it must be admitted that there is also twoness and fourness. Nevertheless, Panikkar maintains that threeness pertains more radically to reality itself.

Wherever we look in the past and around us today, it is evident that there is something beyond what reason and the senses indicate. Magicians, sorcerers, poets and artists, as well as ordinary people, all bear witness to this fact. Moses is described as one who sees the invisible. Panikkar emphasizes that every human person can be the "see-er" of the invisible. Specifically, God is not available to the senses or the intellect. Contemplation is needed; and in the process of contemplation, there is a kind of abandonment of both the senses and the intellect if one is to come into contact with God.

In his discussion of the radical Trinity, Panikkar points out three important aspects of reality. First, reality is not what the senses and the intellect disclose. It is necessary to progress beyond them. Secondly, the "beyond" is neither an entity nor a non-entity. If it were such, then the senses and intellect would be sufficient in their disclosures. Thirdly, true disclosure presupposes a *kenosis*. The human person must undergo an emptying of self in order to experience union with reality. Without this union the experience of trinitarian reality is hampered. Panikkar speaks of this union in terms of a touch. This touch, which is not of the senses or of the intellect, is a substantial one. It is in the touching point that there is no separation of the one thing from the other.

Reality is in the realm of experience. Panikkar's term "experience" means "immediate contact with the real."[52] Human experience and contact with the real occur in three ways: through the senses, the intellect and the mystical faculty. He notes that the mystical faculty has little to do with parapsychology or psychological phenomena, i.e., such things as visions.

Panikkar contends that there is an almost universal witness of human memory that experience is mediated in these three ways which he calls "organs." His description of the role of the three "organs" is said to serve as the background of his treatment of the radical Trinity. He argues that for approaching the real, human beings avail themselves of these three organs or powers or faculties in the following ways.

Regarding the senses, there is awareness that their witnessing is not a sure knowledge of reality. For example, the stick immersed in water appears broken. The senses perceive incorrectly. The mind works on the senses to overcome their misperception and weaknesses. Panikkar points out that the mind allows one to basically trust the senses. The broken stick is not an alarming phenomenon, because the mind enables the person to understand.

Regarding the intellect, Panikkar argues that it too is capable of leading into error, as, for example, in the dichotomous understanding of the relationship between body and soul. Panikkar asks: Who overcomes the contradictions of the mind? He maintains that it is the mystical organ that distinguishes between the real and unreal and allows humans to overcome the mind's contradictions. This would be a scandal only for the rationalists.

It is necessary to function in the realm of faith or myth in order for the mystical faculty to transcend both the senses and reason. All one's organs or powers are needed to distinguish the authentic from the inauthentic. Panikkar claims that, although reason may not be the highest tribunal, it has the first jurisdiction and has the right to send to a possible higher instance those cases that reason itself judges to supersede its competence.[53]

Panikkar holds that, although something may appear to the mind, it does not have to be real. Again, he appeals to the testimony of the common people, pundits and professors to show how this illusion is recognized. What happens in the realm of the mystical or the spiritual has to be final on grounds different from rationality alone. He points out that the spirit[54] does not claim to reduce everything to rationality and consensus. The spirit functions according to its own terms; however, this is understood only by those who have reached the level of the spirit. Panikkar claims that the true dilemma is not between reason and spirit. The two are inseparable; and in fact the three organs or faculties are not really three, because they cannot function independently.

Panikkar admits that in any mystical experience reason and intellect are operative. However, alone they are not adequate for appreciating the fullness of the mystical experience.

The three elements or faculties, i.e., the senses, the intellect and the mystical faculty, must engage in a mutual interplay with an inner harmony of reality, because no one of the three is supreme. Reducing the mystical to the intellectual results in a reductionism which leads to distortion. The spirit cannot be reduced to the *logos*. The word contains more than the words. Panikkar sees the *logos*, the intellectual, as having a mediating role. It is the spirit that breathes through the word and overcomes the contradictions.

The radical Trinity according to Panikkar is not a special revelation. Its reality has been present in the consciousness of people throughout historical memory. Human beings are not alienated spectators or puppets of the divine from above. They are immersed within the reality of the Trinity. In his discussion of the radical Trinity, Panikkar expresses a twofold intention. First, he wishes to present the underlying myth of human experience. Secondly, he desires "to understand, situate and rescue from a provincialistic interpretation the traditional Christian concept of the Trinity."[55]

In carrying out these two intentions, Panikkar claims to reflect the traditional insights of the Christian Trinity and at the same time to expand the traditional insights in order to truly embrace the universal human experience. The radical Trinity as proposed by Panikkar is not synonymous with the traditional understanding of the Trinity. He claims that although his proposal is new, it does not collide with the traditional understanding, because his intention is not to describe the mystery of God. His hope is that his new proposal may eventually be an enlarging and deepening of the doctrine which until now has been solely a Christian preserve. He claims that this integration and expansion will be possible if three conditions are met.

First, this new universal radical Trinity cannot stand in contradiction with Christian tradition as a whole. Secondly, it is necessary for a general Christian vision to open up to a more universal insight. Thirdly, if the radical Trinity is to be called Christian, then it needs to be accepted by the entire Christian community. It cannot be "on one man's shore; it has to be an ecclesial, communitarian affair."[56]

Panikkar in his struggle to develop a universal concept of the Trinity affirms that he is not preoccupied with being orthodox in a confessional sense, nor is he being individualistic. What he is attempting to do is bring out the internal dynamic at work in the universal human experience. He envisions that his radical Trinity may interest and fascinate or, on the other hand, perhaps irritate many within the Christian tradition. It should be noted at this point that Panikkar's treatment of the radical Trinity in this lecture is sketchy and even ambiguous. Most significantly, the question arises whether he actually accomplishes what he has set out to do, i.e., to show how the three organs or faculties serve as the background of his treatment of the radical Trinity.

D. University of Tulsa Warren Lecture: On Catholic Identity (1991)

This work does not refer specifically to Panikkar's trinitarian thought. However, there are some trinitarian implications.

With the development of Panikkar's theology moving in a direction in which the Trinity is seen as a universal concept with concrete reflections in all religions and also within the depth of every individual, even beyond religious settings, four questions emerge.

1. Who is a Christian ?

Panikkar asserts, "A christian is then for me the incarnated person, i.e. the individual in whom the divine spirit has become flesh."[57] However, he makes the following distinctions: a) "the ontic christian, in whom the divine spirit is the living principle"; b) "the ontological christian, in whom there is a certain consciousness of the immanent-transcendent mystery that enlivens one's life"; c) "the historical christian, for whom the christian language makes sense and has been appropriated"; d) "the sociological christian, which I could also call the ecclesiastical one, who owes allegiance to one of the existing christian groups or churches"; e) "the catholic christian, who embodies in a particular way that mysterious consciousness . . ."[58]

For Panikkar Christian identity is determined by the indwelling of Christ's Spirit, that is, the Holy Spirit: "What makes then a christian christian? My answer is simple. Christ's Spirit is the Holy Spirit. This Holy Spirit is the Divine Life. This Divine Life is just the Mystery of Life."[59] But it is significant to remember that for Panikkar "Any human being is a Christian," i.e., an "ontic Christian."[60] There are Christians in

the more restricted senses, listed in the paragraph immediately below, to
the extent that some persons are conscious of the mystery within them.[61]

2. Who is a Catholic?

"A roman catholic . . . [is] the person whose spiritual pedigree passes
through those two million millennia of roman history, not to get entangled
in it or glorify it, but as the springboard from which the christian tradition
may still jump into the Unknown."[62]

Panikkar further elaborates on what it means to be a Roman Catholic:
"To be a catholic, for me, means the conviction, the belief that the Divine
Spirit, similar as in the case of Jesus, has descended over me and has
become incarnated in me, making of me not another Christ (*alter
Christus*), but the same Christ (*ipse Christus*) of which Jesus Christ is
the head (to follow Paul) and I am a member in the process of becoming
it fuller and fuller."[63] What Panikkar here pinpoints as the hallmark of
the Roman Catholic is the "conviction, the beliefs," i.e., the consciousness
of a mystery not necessarily absent in non-Christians. Furthermore, to
distinguish Catholics from other Christians, Panikkar adds: "the catholic
christian . . . embodies in a very particular way that mysterious
consciousness."[64]

3. Who is Jesus Christ?

Although this question is not raised explicit in the work, it is dealt
with obliquely, as Panikkar addresses the issue of Christian identity. There
is a progression in his choice of terminology as he points to Jesus Christ
as the centre of Christianity.

First of all, Panikkar rules out the "teaching or any idea"[65] of Jesus
Christ as the core of Christianity. Secondly, Panikkar offers the
"'person'of Jesus Christ . . . as the center of christianity."[66] Thirdly,
Panikkar explains: "avoiding the concept 'person,' we find the *symbol*
Christ as the very center of christian identity."[67] Fourthly and finally,
"Jesus Christ becomes . . . fundamentally a *historical* symbol. There is
only one (historical) Jesus of Nazareth. History is the matrix of reality.
And in that history Jesus has performed a unique[68] role which is different
from all the other 'manifestations' of the 'Divine.'"[69]

The progression is significant: First, Panikkar asserts that Christianity
cannot be said to focus on the "teaching" of Jesus Christ. It would seem
that he wants to avoid having to deal with certain teachings that may
prove too restrictive for the development of his thought.

For this reason he shifts the expression to the "person" of Jesus Christ as the centre of Christianity. This second expression, the "person" of Jesus Christ, is therefore provisionally preferred as the centre of Christianity. However, even the "person of Jesus Christ" is apparently still inhibitive for Panikkar. It would seem that he has a problem with "Jesus" in other facets of his theology.

Therefore in a third shift, he chooses to avoid the concept "person," and replaces it with "the *symbol* Christ as the very center of Christianity." The shift from "the 'person' of Jesus Christ" to "the *symbol* Christ" is significant as a further weakening of his centrality.

In the fourth and final expression the "*symbol* Christ" becomes "Jesus Christ . . . [as] a *historical* symbol." The progression is complete. Panikkar here is not satisfied with the expression "the symbol Christ," which he will elsewhere equate with the Logos, present also in other manifestations as a universal symbol. Therefore, in order to rule out any "exclusivity or superiority" of Christianity, Panikkar is careful to say that Jesus Christ is only a "*historical* symbol," with a "unique role." However, the uniqueness is a weak one, open to the following interpretation. What Jesus has accomplished is "different from all other 'manifestations' of the divine,"[70] but not in any exclusive or superior way.

4. What is the Significance of the Sacraments?

In his earlier trinitarian and christological thinking, Panikkar clearly recognized the importance of the Sacraments in their traditional understanding,[71] although he had difficulty explaining them in terms of his new thinking. It will be of some interest now to examine what he says about the Sacrament of Baptism in this 1991 work: "This is what is meant by baptism. A christian is a person baptized (in this sense) by the Holy Spirit."[72]

For Panikkar, "baptized in this sense" means that:

> the Divine Spirit, similar as in the case of Jesus, has descended over me and has become incarnated in me, making of me not another Christ . . . but the same Christ . . . of which Jesus Christ is the head . . . and I am a member . . . It means to be an incarnated person, i.e. somebody in whom the divine Spirit dwells not as a host, but as its soul . . . .[73]

However, Panikkar goes on to say that in a sense "any human being . . . is a Christian": "the ontic Christian, in whom the divine spirit is the living principle."[74] It would follow then that the "baptism" that makes one a Christian is not only the Sacrament of Baptism but also baptism in this wider sense. What makes one not only an "ontic Christian" but also a Christian in the other more restricted senses, is the consciousness of this mystery. A "Catholic Christian" is one "who embodies in a particular way that mysterious consciousness."[75]

5. Concluding remarks

Panikkar affirms, "to me my christian consciousness is nothing that severs me from my fellow-beings, but just the contrary, that which establishes the deepest bond of communion, namely that we are pervaded by the divine Spirit . . . "[76]

Being a Christian means belonging to the ultimate sphere.[77] Panikkar's latest thought reflects the universality which he sees as such an important characteristic of the Roman Catholic. "When I confess myself a catholic . . . I am confessing my belonging to the human race, and even more to the entire reality which since eons has taken the shape it has taken in me."[78] For Panikkar, there is a sense in which any human being is Christian ("ontic Christian"): one in whom the Divine Spirit is the living principle.

E. Cardinal Bellarmine Lecture: "A Christophany for Our Times" (1992)[79]

In one of his latest published works, the Cardinal Bellarmine Lecture, Panikkar develops "A Christophany for Our Times." Although in his *Gifford Lectures* of 1989 Panikkar was primarily concerned with a formulation of the Trinity for our times, in this conference delivered two years later he deals with "A Christophany for Our times". The lecture is of significance not only because it represents his latest theology but also because it harks back to the problem that Panikkar faced in his *The Unknown Christ of Hinduism* (1964)[80] and summarizes some of the important conclusions that Panikkar has reached in the latest stage of his journey towards an understanding of the Triune God with insights from universal, non-Christian perspectives.

In an attempt to pursue some of the problems addressed in his earlier thought, Panikkar raises three questions. How do Christians understand Christ? How do non-Christians understand Christ? How do Christians

and non-Christians together understand Christ? He makes nine statements
as a guide for a Christian approach to the third millennium. This section
will highlight elements in the lecture especially pertinent to Panikkar's
trinitarian thought.

First, "Christ is the full manifestation of the Trinity."[82] Panikkar
sees Christ as fundamental to the understanding of the Trinity. It is
through Christ that the Trinity is made known to humanity. Separating
Christ from the Trinity would mean the figure of Christ losing all
credibility.[83]

Secondly, Christ the Logos is not "limited" to the historical Jesus.
"Jesus is the Christ, but the Christ cannot be totally identified with
Jesus."[84] Also, "To say that the 'Jesus of History,' i.e., the Son of Mary,
is the 'Christ of faith,' the 'Son of Man' . . . is precisely the scandal of
christian concreteness which no christian can deny without undermining
the very foundation of Christianity."[85] Panikkar declares that "'The name
above all name' [sic] stands also above the name of Jesus, it is a
supername . . ."[86] According to Panikkar to identify Christ with the
Jesus of history is to limit Christology and may even produce a "Jesus as
messiah"[87] who "is bound to be misunderstood, besides being
alienating"[88] in cultures such as India.

Thirdly, to discover Jesus means experiencing eternal life, which
includes discovering "the reality of matter, of the cosmos."[89] For
Panikkar, Jesus Christ is the symbol not only of divinity and humanity
but also of the cosmos, that is, the material universe.[90]

Panikkar presents Christ as the symbol of all reality. He is "the
symbol of the entire divinization of the universe . . . The entire universe
is called upon to share in the trinitarian *perichoresis*, precisely in and
through Christ."[91]

Fourthly, Panikkar explains that "Christophany makes sense only
within a trinitarian insight."[92] He sees each person as a christophany:
"each being is a christophany, a manifestation of the christic adventure
of all reality on its way towards infinite mystery."[93] For him, Jesus is the
"prototype of all humanity, . . . the full Man."[94]

Fifthly, Panikkar asserts that all reality in Christian terms is "Father,
Christ, and Holy Spirit: the Source of all Being, Being in its Being-ness
(i.e., its Be-coming which is the *Christus totus* not yet fully realized as
long as time lasts), and Spirit (the wind, the energy which maintains this
perichoresis in movement)."[95] Panikkar describes the function of Christ
in terms of Creator, Redeemer and Glorifier.[96]

F. Summary

Panikkar's later thought on the Trinity undergoes continual development and change. In the process of attempting to bridge the gap between Christianity and Hinduism, new ideas emerge in his understanding. His Christology gradually becomes expressed more in terms of a trinitarian theology. His trinitarian concept, although rooted in Christianity, shifts towards an inclusion of categories from the Eastern religious traditions, especially from the Advaita Vedanta school of Hinduism and from Buddhism. This section will briefly summarize Panikkar's later trinitarian theology.

First, borrowing from the school of Buddhism, Panikkar presents the First Person of the Trinity in terms of categories from the Nirvana experience. God, the Father is total non-expression. Everything he is, is expressed through the Son. Although the later Panikkar tends to speak of the Father in terms of the Son, Panikkar does not develop his thought on the First Person of the Trinity. In Panikkar's categories the Father is not spoken of as Creator. He functions through the Son, who is Creator, Redeemer and Sanctifier. The Father pours out all into his Son.

Secondly, the concept of "Christ" in the later writings of Panikkar gradually is distanced from Jesus of Nazareth. There emerges a treatment of the Trinity that exists and functions from within the specific tradition with which Panikkar is dealing. Because his later theology attempts to deal with all non-Christian traditions collectively, he utilizes certain categories that are untraditional in speaking about the Trinity. His notion of Christ is the key and foundational source for proposing and, indeed, stating that the Trinity is manifested in depth in the non-Christian traditions. Therefore the Trinity can be expressed in the Bhakti school or the Advaita tradition without being linked to Jesus Christ or Christianity. Panikkar's later trinitarian thinking also presents a concept of Christ that is intimately connected with every human person, even if that person has no adherence to any religious tradition. The Trinity exists within the innermost being of the individual.

Thirdly, Panikkar's Pneumatology places the experience of the Holy Spirit in the context of non-duality that is operative within the human being. The Spirit functions within the individual in such a manner that enables the person to become aware of the "Christ."

Fourthly, Panikkar's later writings indicate a movement linking Christian categories with those of other religions. He eludicates the relationship among these religions under the umbrella of the Trinity.

However, there is a sense in which he keeps them clearly apart, each with its own unique and authentic experience of God. He describes their relationships in terms of homeomorphic equivalents.

Fifthly, Panikkar's later thought seldom speaks of the Sacraments. However, he would still hold that the Sacraments are valid for the Christian. His references to the Sacraments are limited to Baptism and Eucharist. The later Panikkar makes very little reference to the Sacraments in connection with Hinduism or any other non-Christian tradition.

Notes

2   Panikkar, *Unknown Christ of Hinduism* (1981), 60.

3   *Ibid.*, 161.

4   *Ibid.*

5   See Frank Whaling, "The Trinity and Structure of Religious Life," in *Christianity and the Religions of the East*, Richard Rousseau, ed. (Scranton: Ridge Row Press, 1982), 45. See also Troy Organ, "Some Contributions of Hinduism to Christianity," *ibid.*, 25. In addition, the Hindu concept of Trimurti is sometimes used by scholars when making comparison within the Trinity. Panikkar, however, does not resort to Trimurti, which is only very loosely analogous to Trinity.

6   Although Saccidananda often describes Brahman in Vedantic philosophy, it does not appear in any of the principal Upanishads. However, Brahman is often expressed in them by separate terms, such as Reality (Sat), Consciousness (Cit) or Bliss (Ananda).

7   Panikkar, *Unknown Christ of Hinduism* (1981), 162.

8   *Ibid.*

9   *Ibid.*

10   The ultimacy of Saccidananda Brahman cannot be an object of formal devotion, but it gives reality to the Gods. Brahman, the Absolute, that people cannot know in a concrete manner, is in reality the inner substance of the Gods. It is through the Gods that one arrives at Brahman; yet it is necessary in Advaita Vedanta thought to move beyond the concrete manifestation of the Gods to be in true union with Brahman.

11   Panikkar, *Unknown Christ of Hindusim* (1981), 53.

12   *Ibid.*, 152.

13   *Ibid.*

14   *Ibid.*

15   *Ibid.*, 154.

16   *Ibid.*, 162.

17   See *ibid.*, 156.

18   *Ibid.*, 49.

19   See *ibid.*, 57.

20   *Ibid.*, 54.

21   *Ibid.*, 49.

22   See *ibid.*, *passim*.

23   *Ibid.* (1964), 26.

24   *Ibid.* (1981), 60.

25   *Ibid.*, 60.

26   *Ibid.* (1964).

27   *Ibid.*, 24.

28   *Ibid.* (1981), 57.

29   *Ibid.*

30   Divine power, creative energy of God.
31   Panikkar, *Unknown Christ of Hinduism* (1981), 57.
32   See *ibid.*, 93-94. See also 93, n. 129.
33   *Ibid.* (1964), ix.
34   *Ibid.* (1981), 93
35   See *ibid.*, 6. (The words, "fullness of God that can be realized," are a paraphrase).
36   *Ibid.* (1981), 6.
38   Panikkar, "The Jordan, the Tiber, and the Ganges," 110.
39   *Ibid.*, 109.
40   *Ibid.*, 109-110.
41   Here Panikkar is not speaking specifically of the Advaita Vedanta tradition of Hinduism but in terms of the non-dualistic experience.
42   Panikkar, "The Jordan, the Tiber, and the Ganges," 110.
43   *Ibid.*
44   *Ibid.*, 111.
45   *Ibid.*, 112.
46   *Ibid.*
47   *Ibid.*
48   *Ibid.*, 113.
49   Comment made to the author in an interview in Tavertet, Spain, in August 1990.
50   The term is Panikkar's: methodic instead of methodology. Panikkar intends to indicate a unique meaning, free from the baggage associated with the word "methodology."
52   Panikkar, "The Radical Trinity," *Gifford Lecture*, No. 6.
53   See *ibid.*
54   Panikkar's use of the word "spirit" in this lecture is very vague and ambiguous.
55   Panikkar, "The Radical Trinity," *Gifford Lecture*, No. 6.
56   *Ibid.*
57   Panikkar, *On Catholic Identity*, 17.
58   *Ibid.*
59   *Ibid.*
60   *Ibid.*
61   This development of Panikkar's thought seems very close to Karl Rahner's "Anonymous Christians." See Karl Rahner's, "Anonymous Christians," *Theological Investigation VI. More Recent Writings*, trans. Kevin Smith (Baltimore: Helicon Press, 1969), 390-398.
62   Panikkar, *On Catholic Identity*, 17.

63 *Ibid.*
64 *Ibid.*
65 *Ibid.*, 7.
66 *Ibid.*
67 *Ibid.*
68 The question arises for the reader: How is the "unique role" of Jesus to be understood? In this particular work Panikkar does not give a complete answer. However, in the light of his other writings it seems that he could be interpreted as saying that Jesus' role is unique to Christianity in the same way as Isvara's role is to Advaitin Hinduism or as Buddha's role is to Buddhism.
69 Panikkar, *On Catholic Identity*, 9.
70 *Ibid.*
71 See, for example, Panikkar, *Unknown Christ of Hindusim* (1964), 60 (on Baptism) and 21 (on Eucharist).
72 Panikkar, *On Catholic Identity*, 17.
73 *Ibid.*
74 *Ibid.*
75 *Ibid.*
76 *Ibid.*, 18.
77 See *ibid.*
78 *Ibid.*
80 Panikkar describes the lecture as "a condensed summary of my christological opinions about which I have written extensively . . . in my scattered writings." *Ibid.*, 21, n. 1.
82 Panikkar, "A Christophany for Our Times," 14.
83 See *ibid.*, 21.
84 *Ibid.*, 9.
85 *Ibid.*
86 *Ibid.*, 11.
87 *Ibid.*, 10.
88 *Ibid.*
89 *Ibid.*, 20.
90 See *ibid.*
91 *Ibid.*, 6.
92 *Ibid.*, 14.
93 *Ibid.*, 7.
94 *Ibid.*, 20.
95 *Ibid.*, 7.
96 See *ibid.*, 14.

Chapter IV

Résumé and Evaluation

Section A of this chapter will summarize the continuity and shifts in Panikkar's trinitarian thought. First, they will be synopsized from the perspective of the development that is evident from the 1964 to the 1981 edition of *The Unknown Christ of Hinduism*. Secondly, the continuity and shifts between Panikkar's earlier and later trinitarian doctrine in general will be recapitulated.

Section B of this chapter will provide an evaluation of Panikkar's trinitarian theology from four perspectives. The first will critique his methodology in light of the factors of theology. The second will review the appraisal of Panikkar by other authors. The third will evaluate the continuity and shifts in his trinitarian concept. The fourth will assess his overall proposal.

A. *Résumé*

1. Continuity and Shifts in Panikkar's Thought From the 1964 to 1981 Edition of The Unknown Christ of Hinduism

The most striking difference between these two texts is found in their orientations. The 1964 edition attempts to establish the universality of the Triune God in Hinduism. Christianity is viewed as the religion where God is manifested fully in Christ. It is the "Truth of religion,"[1] while Hinduism, the "Religion of truth"[2] posesses this "hidden" Christ in the expression of Isvara. Christianity is already the resurrected religion; Hinduism is still in need of this rebirth.

The 1981 edition seeks to retain the substance of the earlier edition while addressing a two-fold concern: first, the criticism of readers; secondly, the need to modify the text so that it will reflect his new ideas on the Triune God.

In both editions the Trinity is "Father, Logos and Holy Spirit."[3] Borrowing from both Christianity and Hinduism, Panikkar declares that everything is God. Both texts are almost identical.

> All that *is*, the whole of Reality, is nothing but God: Father, Christ and Holy Spirit.[4]

> All that exists, i.e. the whole reality, is nothing but God: Father, Christ and Holy Spirit.[5]

Panikkar refers to the Trinity also as follows:

> In him [Christ] all is recapitulated and the Spirit will quicken it with that life which overflows out of the Father alone.[6]

> In him all things are summed up and the Spirit will quicken them with that life which flows out of the Father alone.[7]

a) *The First Person of the Trinity*

In both editions the concept of God the Father remains essentially the same. When Panikkar speaks of God from the Indian perspective of Brahman, he is referring to what he would also call God the Father. The following two passages remain the same in both editions, except that in the later edition Panikkar prefers to not mention Nirguna Brahman.

> There is Brahman, or God, or the godhead as the absolute and in consequence unrelated, unchangeable,   unique, simple - really nirguna.[8]

> There is Brahman, or God, or the Divinity as Absolute, without relation, immutable, unique, simple.[9]

Also Panikkar states that God the Father is the source of the whole Divinity in both his early and later editions of *The Unknown Christ of Hinduism.*[10] That the Father is expressed totally in the Son is also common to both editions.

b) *Second Person of the Trinity*

Between the 1964 and the 1981 editions of *The Unknown Christ of Hindusim*, several comparisons emerge. First, in the 1964 edition Christianity is seen as the "fullness of religion" and the real "per-fection of every religion."[11] In the 1981 edition these comments are eliminated.

Secondly, in the earlier edition, Christ has "unveiled his whole face" in Christianity; however, in Hinduism his mission is still incomplete, "Christ has not unveiled his whole face . . . "[12] In the later edition this distinction disappears.

Thirdly, in the earlier edition, Hinduism is presented as a "kind of Christianity in potency" because it is the "desire of fullness, and that fullness is Christ . . . "[13] In the later edition, Hinduism is presented as equally authentic as Christianity. The fullness of Christ is manifested equivalently in both traditions.

Fourthly, in the 1964 edition Panikkar is careful to nuance his statements regarding Hinduism or any other non-Christian tradition regarding the extent to which Christ is present. Regarding Hinduism he states:

> Christ is already there in Hinduism in so far as Hinduism is a true religion; Christ is already at work in any Hindu prayer as far as it is really prayer."[14]

His 1981 edition, however, is less nuanced. He eliminates the need for any conditions to be fulfilled. The paragraph is therefore revised to read as follows:

> Christ is already present in Hinduism. The Spirit of Christ is already at work in Hindu prayers.[15]

Christ's presence in Hinduism is boldly asserted. His presence is not subject to the two conditions stipulated in the earlier edition, i.e., first, the extent to which Hinduism is a true religion and secondly, the extent to which Hindu prayer is really prayer.

Fifthly, the 1964 description of the Logos is traditional. The Logos becomes man in Jesus of Nazareth. The 1981 edition, however, speaks of the Logos in terms that are more radical: the "Logos is Man." To be noted is the difference in the two editions: man (1964) and Man (1981).

> And again faith will let me into the unfathomable womb of the divinity and make me discover, realise, that this father is all-powerful, creator . . . and the Logos became man . . . and the Spirit breathes in his Church . . . [16]

> And faith in turn allows me to enter into the ineffable heart of Divinity, there to discover, to understand that this Father is omnipotent, creator; and that the Logos is Man, and that the Spirit is the living breath of his People and of the universe . . . [17]

Sixthly, in the earlier edition Christ is very much present in the Sacraments:

> Simply because Christ is fully present in the eucharist and the eucharist has been entrusted to the Church, Hinduism also has a right to have it, which comes to mean that Christianity has not the right to keep it for itself, but must offer it even to the Hindu.[18]

In the 1981 edition this sentence is eliminated completely. There is no reason to question that Panikkar would still hold that Christ is fully present in the Eucharist. However, in his later edition Panikkar prefers not to highlight the Sacraments or the "full Presence of Christ" in Christianity.

c) *Third Person of the Trinity*

There are several additional shifts in Panikkar's trinitarian thought from his earlier edition to his later one.

First, there is a shift in emphasis from Christ to the Holy Spirit as the meeting point between Christians and Hindus.[19]

Secondly, there is a further emphasis in the later edition on the Spirit as the main presence associated with the experience of Advaita, i.e., non-duality. It is through the experience of non-duality that the Advaitin comes to experience the Trinity.

Thirdly, the Spirit becomes increasingly more important as Panikkar moves from the earlier to the later edition, although the Spirit is still basically formulated within traditional trinitarian thought. In both editions, the Trinity is "Father, Logos and Holy Spirit."[20]

Fourthly, the major change in Panikkar's thought is the shift from "the Spirit breathes in his Church"[21] to "the Spirit is the living breath of his People and of the universe."[22] Although the new formulation is traditional in itself, taken in the context of Panikkar's trinitarian thought, the subtle change is highly significant. Here there is also a further shift in Panikkar's meaning of Church.

Fifthly, in the earlier edition, the Holy Spirit is important to the sacramental life of the individual. "One has to be reborn in water, blood and Holy Spirit to the new Christian existence."[23] In the later edition this and most other references to the Sacraments are eliminated; however, Panikkar would hold that the Holy Spirit is still important to the "sacramental" life of the individual, but in a totally new sense. The Spirit still "makes all things new."[24]

2. Continuity and Shifts in Panikkar's Overall Thought on Trinity

Panikkar's trinitarian thought undergoes major changes from his earlier writings to the later ones. These changes in his thinking are expressed not in terms of abrupt differences involving dramatic shifting of gears. Instead, the differences are present in very subtle ways, but often with deep repercussions.

This section will distill the principal examples of continuity and shifts in his trinitarian thought during the many years of struggling to shed light on the experience of the Trinity in other religious traditions, especially Hinduism, while still attempting to retain and even deepen his faith in Christ and Christianity. Panikkar's considerable departure from traditional church teaching in his later trinitarian thought is seminally present in the earlier stage. His attitude during the period in which his thought is undergoing substantial change is always accompanied by deep faith and a genuine search for ways in which to express the universal gift of the Trinity.

There are areas in which Panikkar exhibits clear continuity in his trinitarian thought. There are other areas of only apparent continuity together with deep, if subtle, changes or shifts. What follows is a five-point summary of continuity and shifts in Panikkar's trinitarian thought.

First, Panikkar moves from a traditional christocentric understanding of the Trinity, with Jesus Christ as central, to what Panikkar claims to be still a christocentric understanding, but which really bypasses Jesus of Nazareth as the discloser of the Trinity for non-Christians. There is a shifting of emphasis from the centrality of the Jesus of history to the "Christs" of the many religions, that is, the Christ of faith expressed as the homeomorphic equivalent within the different traditions.

Secondly, Panikkar shifts his emphasis from the Roman Catholic Church to the "world" Church. He would hold that he has always believed in the universality of the Church. However, in his trinitarian theology, there is a shift from emphasizing a presence of the Spirit within the Church in a special way to a presence within the "world Church," i.e., within each human person, regardless of religion. Panikkar never really denies that the Spirit is present in the Roman Catholic or Christian Church in a special way. In fact, there is no doubt Panikkar still holds this. However, in his attempt to break down the barriers of organized religion, including the walls that he claims imprison the Trinity within the confines of Christianity, he centres the activity of the Spirit within the human person. For Panikkar, it is the building up of the human person universally that constitutes the authentic Church.

Thirdly, Panikkar proposes in his later thought a concept of the Trinity that is centred, not on revelation through Jesus Christ, but on the Advaitin tradition of Hinduism. Even in Panikkar's earlier thought, in which the Nirvana experience in Buddhism reflects the experience of the First Person of the Trinity and in which the Christian experience of Jesus in Christianity reflects the experience of the Second Person of the Trinity, the Advaitin experience is seen as reflecting not only the experience of the Third person of the Trinity but also the experience of the whole Trinity.

Even in Panikkar's earlier trinitarian thought the Nirvana experience of God as ineffable (*neti, neti*: not this, not that) can be experienced also in the Advaita Vedanta tradition. Also, even when Jesus in Christianity reflects the experience of the Second Person of the Trinity, Jesus is only one of many. Within Hinduism the Bhakti tradition also typifies the experience of the Second Person of the Trinity. Also in his earlier writings, e.g., in *The Unknown Christ of Hinduism* (1964), the Second Person of the Trinity is seen in terms of Isvara. Granted that the earlier Panikkar is trying to bridge the gap between Christianity and Hinduism, while utilizing concepts from Buddhism in the process, he centres more and more on the Advaitin tradition in the development of his trinitarian thought.

This is important because, although it was not Panikkar's intention to develop a trinitarian concept out of any one tradition, he actually starts with the Advaitin position as central to the trinitarian experience. In the Advaitin tradition the Mandukya Upanishads indicate that "everything is Aum" and that every human person is destined towards the experience of Self-Realization.[25] The later Panikkar emphasizes where the experience of the Divine is everywhere a trinitarian experience; the entire world is sacred space; and every human being in the universe is a participant in the "Trinitarian Reality."

Fourthly, Panikkar expresses himself in a style that becomes more and more Eastern as his trinitarian thought develops. His earlier clarity, precision, definitive parameters, rootedness in history and immersion in a set tradition give way to an approach that is equally valid but bears the aura of the East. It is universality that prevails. The human person looms foremost as a participant in the trinitarian life.

The later Panikkar removes the "shackles" of religion so that the Trinity may becomes a Reality in experience, regardless of religious structures. In the *Gifford Lectures* (1989)[26] Panikkar views monotheism as an obstruction to faith and to participation in the communitarian relationship existing between the Trinity and all human beings.[27] Jesus is good for Christians. God from the Christian perspective is good for Christians. Allah is good for Moslems. However, a truly universal God including a *neti, neti* (not this, not that) "God," as in the case of Buddhism, requires something more than what monotheism has produced historically. For the universal Trinity to become known and experienced by all of humanity, traditional concepts of God must give way to something radically new. Panikkar's cosmotheandrism and christophany point to new horizons but appear inadequate. This radically new aspect may seem valid; however, its Eastern lack of clarity and of clear definition prevails in the later trinitarian thought of Raimon Panikkar.

Fifthly, there is a development in Panikkar's trinitarian reflection from the viewpoint of his overall orientation. He avails himself of the traditional Christian concept of the Trinity and maps out two possiblities of speaking about the Trinity in the context of other religions. Two frameworks emerge in his thinking almost simultaneously: Trinity and Advaita in *The Unknown Christ of Hinduism* (1964); and Trinity and the spiritualities of the world religions seen in *The Trinity and the Religious Experience of Man* (1973).[28] Although the development of his thought pulled him in the direction of a new Christology, Panikkar's took refuge in a trinitarian theology to justify his non-traditional Christology.

The final conclusion of his trinitarian theology is difficult to concretize in words. This is partly because in the last phase of his trinitarian thinking, Panikkar feels the need to break with religion in general. The secular world became a dominant force in Panikkar's later discourse on the Trinity. The later Panikkar left himself no other alternative but to centre the Trinity within the human person seeking and being sought by the Divine.

B. Evaluation

1. Critique of Panikkar's Methodology in Light of the Formative Factors of Theology

The following section will present an evaluation of Panikkar's methodology[29] based on Macquarrie's "formative factors of theology" with the addition of magisterium and liturgy.

a) Experience

As indicated earlier,[30] experience looms large for Panikkar throughout the development of his trinitarian theology. He categorizes experience as the foundation of all that can be said about the Blessed Trinity. Although for the earlier Panikkar, experience is rooted in Jesus of Nazareth and within the parameters of the Roman Catholic Church, there is a gradual shift; and it remains unclear whether in his latest works Panikkar still finds the experience of Jesus Christ as fundamental to his own experience of the Trinity in spite of the fact that he still functions as a Roman Catholic priest. As his experience became wider and varied, a change occurred in his beliefs, even in his adherence to some basic tenets of Christianity. He states in a recent (1988) letter, "There has been evolution in my ideas, . . . and eventually also some kind of mutation."[31] It is obvious that Panikkar considers this mutation as an enhancement of his penetration of the Trinity.

As for the Hindu, Buddhist or even the person who does not adhere to any religious tradition, Panikkar would claim that they all have other experiential doors to the Trinity. Although these doors come collectively under the umbrella of "Christ," they differ widely and dramatically from the categories of experience that have dominated Christian theology for two millenia. Panikkar's universal framework of Trinity draws heavily on the experience of Hinduism and Buddhism. He sees his understanding of the Trinity as vastly enriched by Hinduism's Advaita and Bhakti traditions, on the one hand, and Buddhism's category of Nirvana, on the other.

The question arises: Is this a valid methodology for a Christian theologian? First of all, Panikkar's insistence on experience of God, wherever it is found, is to be applauded. This is the starting point, at least implicitly for any theologizing. Secondly, his drawing on Hinduism and Buddhism is also to be appreciated. Methodologically, this is a good beginning. The crucial question is whether or not the content of his trinitarian thought has been unduly influenced by his attempt to incorporate Hindu and Buddhist elements into his trinitarian synthesis. As has been evident throughout this study, the present writer would answer affirmatively, although one must praise Panikkar's pioneering attempt to enrich the Christian understanding of Trinity with insights from other religious traditions.

b) Revelation

Raimon Panikkar's use of revelation in the development of his trinitarian understanding is central. The earlier Panikkar focused on Christian revelation as he attempted to expand the horizon and depth of the Christian concept of the Trinity. At the same time he took seriously revelation as present in other religions as well, especially Hinduism and Buddhism. The later Panikkar, however, shifted his position as his trinitarian thought underwent further development. Christian revelation is no longer in any way the fullness of God's disclosure. Although Panikkar still maintains the word "Christ" as a central factor, in his trinitarian theology the word "Christ" has taken on a wider meaning; and revelation is recognized almost equally in other religions and even beyond the boundaries of any religion, in the depth of the human person.

The evaluation of Panikkar's methodolody with regard to revelation as a formative factor of theology will be approached in two steps: a positive assessment and a negative one.

First, Panikkar's treatment of revelation generally proceeds very soundly from the viewpoint of methodology. He does treat revelation "as the primary source of theology."[32] As one would expect from a Christian theologian, he appeals primarily to Christian revelation with Jesus Christ as *the* bearer of revelation, at least in his earlier works. Also, in keeping with mainline Christian thinking, Panikkar acknowledges divine revelation outside of Christianity, i.e., as taking place in other religions and even beyond the realm of any religion.

Secondly, in his later works Panikkar's methodological treatment of revelation is flawed in at least two respects from the viewpoint of Christian theology. First, Jesus Christ gradually recedes as "the fullness of all revelation."[33]   Secondly, Panikkar's employment of the term "Christ" in his later works to denote other "incarnations" and homeomorphic equivalents of the Second Person of the Trinity appears to be an unwarranted tampering with established terminology in Christian theology beyond any acceptable usage of "communicatio idiomatum."

c) Scripture

Panikkar's use of Scripture is fairly extensive throughout the development of his trinitarian theology. Because his earlier thought was more grounded in the traditional Christian concept of the Trinity, his employment of Christian Scripture, both Old and New Testaments, is more prevalent. His earliest writings also indicate an attempt to draw on scriptural sources from other religions. Panikkar's later writings have continued to make use of numerous scriptural sources, both Christian and non-Christian, to substantiate his new ideas. The evaluation of Panikkar's trinitarian methodology with regard to scripture as a formative factor of theology will be addressed from two viewpoints: Christian Scriptures, including both Old and New Testaments; and the Scriptures of other religions, particularly Hinduism.

First, Panikkar constantly uses the Christian Scriptures, especially the books of the New Testament, with special reference to the Gospels and the Pauline corpus. He does so with thoroughness and respect, especially in his earlier writings. However, it would not be unfair to add that his exegesis does not always reflect the mainstream of Christian biblical scholarship. Of course, the content of his later thinking has a reciprocal effect on how he interprets the Christian Scriptures, that is, in an increasingly original way.

Secondly, Panikkar deserves high praise for generally taking seriously the sacred books of other religions. In this respect the judgement of John Macquarrie applies favorably to Panikkar: "We are all agreed that theology must keep in close touch with its biblical sources, but to try to exclude non-biblical sources is absurd."[34]

As for Buddhism, even Panikkar's employment over the years of such concepts as Nirvana in his trinitarian theology gives very little evidence of any close contact with the Buddhist Scriptures. Even his excellent work, *The Silence of God*, when speaking of Buddhism and the Trinity, surprisingly fails to explore the Buddhist Scriptures in any depth.[35]

As for Hinduism, it is here that Panikkar is to be especially applauded for his openness, courage and creativity in seeking to understand the Trinity with the help of non-Christian scripture sources. However, what is suprising throughout the development of Panikkar's thought on the Trinity from 1957 to 1993 is his limited use of the Manduyka Upanishad. Although references are made to this Upanishad, which is the basis of the Advaita school of Hinduism, Panikkar never gives a clear comprehensive breakdown of what this Upanishad is saying. Because this Upanishad is short and the Advaita thought permeates his entire trinitarian theology from its earliest beginnings to its latest stage, it would appear that he should have given it considerably much more attention. Panikkar, however, does draw on many of the other Hindu scriptural sources, both from the Vedas as well as the Upanishads.

Because the Manduyka Upanishad does not receive a fuller treatment, the reader is left with the impression that the Advaita experience simply reflects non-duality. It is to be granted that Advaita means non-duality. Nevertheless, it is by going back to the Hindu Scriptures, specifically the Manduyka Upanishad, that one realizes that there is a process of experiencing that takes place before the experience of non-duality within the Advaita school of Hinduism. This critique leveled at Panikkar regarding the employment of this Scripture stems from the way he presents the Advaita experience: he gives an inadequate idea of what that school teaches through its primary Scripture, the Manduyka Upanishad.

Despite the limitations of Panikkar's use of the non-Christian Scriptures, they have been very helpful to him in understanding the experience of God, or of the Ultimate, in the world religions.

d) Tradition

Panikkar's use of tradition permeates the development of his trinitarian thought. His universal concept of Trinity is based not only on the original Christian revelation but also on the experience and writings of the Greek Fathers and the early Franciscan School.[36]

Panikkar, however, does not limit himself to Christian tradition. He makes use also of the traditions of various non-Christian religious cultures. As a result he has introduced into his theology of Trinity new ideas: religious symbols, myths and other categories throughout history. For example, observing the development of the role of Isvara in the traditions of Hinduism,[37] he feels justified in continuing the development and in declaring that Isvara is "Christ."

When Panikkar's employment of tradition as a formative factor in his trinitarian methodology was treated earlier,[38] a question remained: Does he sufficiently avoid the extreme of breaking with trinitarian tradition for the sake of being relevant? The answer seems clear. He appears to have taken great pains to maintain the trinitarian tradition, while universalizing the notion of Trinity. It is another question whether he has in the process not radically departed from christological tradition.

Panikkar's contact with the traditions of the world religions has provided a healthy graft onto the tree of Christian trinitarian theology. The present writer would basically concur in the perhaps slightly hyperbolic judgement of Ewert Cousins on the direction of Panikkar's trinitarian theology: "In the encounter with world religions I foresee a development of the doctrine of Trinity comparable to the one that occurred in the Golden Age of the Greek Fathers and in the High Middle Ages of the West."[39]

e) Culture

Panikkar deeply reflects the role of culture throughout his trinitarian writings. He addresses not only cultures from which the great world religions have emerged but also cultures in the secular world, with or without religious structures.

Although it is only his later trinitarian thinking that addresses explicity non-religious cultures, his earlier thought centering the experience of the Trinity within the human person, whether Christian or not, was really a forerunner of his later theology that has moved unabashedly into the arena of the secular world.

The earlier Panikkar tends to focus on the integration and assimilation of other cultures into a concept of Trinity that tries to embrace all cultures. The later Panikkar in his treatment of Trinity is more inclined to emphasize the uniqueness of individuals rather than integration and assimilation into the Christian concept of Trinity.

Culture is perhaps the most operative of the formative factors in Panikkar's trinitarian theology. He restates the doctrine of the Trinity in terms of Eastern culture a) in order to make the doctrine more relevant to the Eastern mind and b) in order for the Christian to understand Trinity in an even deeper way. The question arises: Has Panikkar maintained the fine balance between the demand for relevance and intelligibility, on the one hand, and the need for truth and continuity, on the other?

Panikkar tries to do just that. However, he is reacting to what he perceives to have been almost two millenia of expression of trinitarian theology exclusively in cultural expressions of the West. In his pioneering effort to give expression to Trinity in Eastern categories he may appear to be veering away from the pole of truth and continuity. However, this is the lot of one who sails unchartered waters. Creative theologians must be allowed flexibility as long as they are open to the reactions of their theological peers and the magisterium. Panikkar acquits himself quite well in this area.

f) Reason

Reason is a most important factor in Panikkar's trinitarian methodology. His use of reason will be evaluated against the background of Macquarrie's distinctions explained above. Reason is divided into speculative (including architectonic) and critical. Critical reason is subdivided into elucidatory and corrective.

Panikkar vigorously employs the various types of reason in his trinitarian theologizing: architectonic, elucidatory and corrective. Of the three, architectonic reason is embraced most vigorously: his trinitarian thought progresses not so much by deductive argument as by imaginative leaps. In his earlier period the Trinity is treated through careful use of reason. In his later period reason is somewhat downplayed: it is not the highest tribunal, although it still enjoys the first jurisdiction and has the right to refer to a possible higher instance those cases that reason itself judges to supersede its competence.[43] In order to experience the Trinity, contact with reality is required through the senses, the intellect and the mystical faculty. Paradoxically, it is through reason that the role of reason is somewhat lessened.

Evaluation of Panikkar's use of reason in his trinitarian methodology must ultimately be a very positive one. Only a subtle penetrating mind could construct such an ingenious framework. However, it must always be remembered that Panikkar is half Indian and that the Indian use of reason is not identical to the European.

g) Magisterium

As a Roman Catholic theologian, Panikkar's use of the magisterium in the development of his trinitarian theology is surprisingly scant. He does give evidence of a good basic knowledge of Church teaching. However, the magisterium plays no vital role in the development of his thought.

Nostra Aetate, the Vatican II Declaration on the Relationship of the Church to Non-Christian Religions, would be problematic for Panikkar even in his earlier writings. Although at times he makes reference to documents issued by the magisterium, he does not deal with them at any length. However, this is understandable, given the nature of his trinitarian enterprise: exploratory, tentative, innovative.

h) Liturgy

In Panikkar's writings on the Trinity the Christian liturgy is given very little attention. In his early works, especially *The Unknown Christ of Hinduism* (1964), and even less in his later works, Panikkar makes several references to the Sacraments, although not in the context of the liturgy.

As indicated above, he addresses the issue of worship in two major works,[45] both from the viewpoint of Hinduism. However, in neither work does he deal in any way with trinitarian themes.

In evaluating Panikkar's neglect of liturgy as a formative factor in his trinitarian methodology, one can be indulgent. Panikkar should not be faulted for not having done everything well: "Ars longa, vita brevis." On the other hand, one can only lament this omission and speculate about the missed opportunities of enhancing his trinitarian corpus with insights from the forms of worship of both Christianity and Hinduism.

2. Critique by Other Authors

This section, dealing with authors who evaluate Panikkar, will be divided into three parts: positive, negative and mixed criticisms.

First, the positive comments and critiques. a) There are many authors who praise Panikkar for his theology in general. Strolz is typical. He lauds Panikkar as a writer who has combined "thinker and religious person . . . into a seldon seen unity . . . "[46] b) Many authors evaluate Panikkar very positively also for his contribution to interfaith dialogue. Baumer-Despeigne is a typical example. In praising Panikkar's general interfaith attitude, she writes, "Only when the partners dare to look into the further heights can they become real partners in intrareligious dialogue, and interreligious dialogue is and should always be intrareligious dialogue as Raimundo Panikkar maintains."[47]

A second author with glowing praise for Panikkar's contribution to interfaith dialogue is Nalini Devdas, who singles out the potential of Panikkar's concept of theandrism for fruitful dialogue: "theandrism participates in the aspiration towards a rich, many-dimensioned spiritual experience which is discovered to be a powerful aspect within every religious tradition . . . Theandrism can encourage fruitful dialogue between those who are committed to integral spirituality and those who find it impossible."[48]

A third writer who applauds Panikkar for his interfaith insights is Anthony Kelly. He refers to Panikkar as one of those who have provided us with "informed and sensitive scholarship."[49] Citing Panikkar's earlier trinitarian framework, Kelly remarks, "This deeply interior experience of the Spirit is something that the classic Hindu experience of self-realization can teach us."[50]

A fourth author who hails Panikkar's contributions in the area of interfaith dialogue is James Kodera, who singles out Panikkar's *The Unknown Christ of Hinduism* as an indicator of the future direction of interreligious dialogue.[51]

A fifth author with a positive judgement of Panikkar's position on interreligious dialogue is Rowan Williams. Responding to the objection that certain Christian doctrines such as The Trinity are absolute obstacles to interfaith relations, he invokes Panikkar as a source of rebuttal. According to Williams, "If Panikkar is right in seeing Trinitarian Christianity as the proper foundation for an interreligious engagement that is neither vacuous nor imperialist, the doctrines of Christian credal orthodoxy are not, as is regularly supposed, insuperable obstacles to dialogue; the incarnation of the logos is not the ultimate assertion of privilege and exclusively, but the center of that network of relations (implicit and explicit) in which a new humanity is to be created."[52] Williams acknowledges that "Panikkar does an exceptional service to authentic engagement between traditions *in* their particularity, in a way not to be found among programmatic relativists."[53]

A sixth and final author with a most positive attitude regarding Panikkar's contribution to interfaith dialogue is Paul Knitter, who has studied Panikkar extensively. Panikkar's trinitarian theology calls for pluralism according to Paul Knitter. In his discussion of Panikkar, Knitter states, "Panikkar is affirming, on the basis of his knowledge of religions and his own religious experience, that the mystery within all religions is both *more than* and yet *has its being* within the diverse experiences and beliefs of the religions."[54] For Panikkar, at the heart of every authentic religion is the trinitarian experience. This conviction accounts, therefore, directly for his insistence on pluralism.

Describing Panikkar's thought on the Ultimate in world religions, Knitter explains:

For him, the Ultimate is not only ineluctably ineffable, it is also radically pluralistic. So too is all reality. Panikkar maintained that even those endorsing a new pluralism and plunging across the Rubicon do not really know what this means. Pluralism tells us that there is no "one" that can be imposed on the "many." There will always be many; there will always be difference and disagreement. The incommensurability of ultimate systems is unbridgeable, and we have to live with this incompatibility not as a lesser evil . . . but as a revelation itself of the nature of reality.[55]

After a review of the positive comments of several representative authors on the trinitarian theology of Raimon Panikkar, this section will summarize the views of three writers who comment negatively on Panikkar's trinitarian theology, and derivatively, on his Christology and pluralistic position.

The first is Gavin D'Costa. He critiques several writers, including Panikkar, who contributed to *The Myth of Christian Uniqueness*. D'Costa maintains that their concerns "are better met by an appropriate doctrine of the Trinity, than by the various strategies they employ, which either ignore, abandon, or under-utilize this most central Christian doctrine of God."[56] Although this statement is not directed specifically at Panikkar, he is included.

The second author who negatively critiques Panikkar is Claude Geffré.[57]

He echoes the strongest and most common criticism of Panikkar, the notion that there can be many Saviours and that Jesus is not "equal" to Christ. Geffré claims that Panikkar has gone too far in his claim that Jesus does not exhaust Christ the Logos: "Je n'irai pas jusqu'à dire comme Raymond Panikkar que le Jésus historique n'épuise pas le Christ-Logos, mais comme je l'ai écrit ailleurs, il me semble légitime de reconnaître que l'humanité de Jésus de Nazareth n'épuise pas le mystère du Christ dans sa préexistence éternelle à la fois comme Dieu et comme homme."[58]

The third and final author chosen from those who find fault with Panikkar is Jacques Dupuis. His *Jesus Christ at the Encounter of World Religions* devotes four pregnant pages to Panikkar in a section entitled "Christ with or without Jesus?"[59] Addressing the question of the relationship between the Jesus of history and the Christ of faith, Dupuis contends that the problem arises only in the later development of Panikkar's thought. Dupuis admits readily that in the 1964 edition of *The Unknown Christ of Hinduism* "there is no reason to suspect . . . any loosening of the bond between Christ and Jesus of Nazareth."[60] Addressing Panikkar's subsequent development, Dupuis claims, "Raimundo Panikkar's thought does not appear to preserve the indissoluble link between the Christ of faith and the Jesus of history. It betrays this link, weakening it and threatening . . . to reduce the Christian message to a kind of gnosis."[61]

Furthermore, Dupuis agrees with the critique of Panikkar by Robert Smet. Dupuis quotes Smet, "The Christian can perfectly well admit a presence of the *Logos* outside of the Christian and Jewish traditions, but is not disposed to believe that the *Logos* acts elsewhere in identical fashion."[62]

After a review, first, of some favourable critiques of Panikkar's theology in the area of Trinity and related topics, and secondly, of some unfavourable critiques, this third section will summarize three mixed critiques, taken in chronological order.

The first author to be considered is Ewert Cousins, who has made a lifelong study of Panikkar. Cousins provides the first comprehensive critique of Panikkar's trinitarian theology.[63]

As for positive evaluation, beginning from 1970 Cousins hails Panikkar's trinitarian construct as "mature" and of immense value. He views Panikkar's trinitarian framework as having an affinity with the trinitarian thought of the Greek Fathers and the early Franciscan school.[64] According to Cousins, Panikkar's main contribution in this respect is his concept of the Father which he links with the spirituality represented by the concept of Nirvana in Buddhism. Cousins affirms that Panikkar's "chief point of originality is his notion of the silence of the Father, which is derived from his immersion in the strong apophatism of Buddhism."[65] With regard to Panikkar's trinitarian concept in the context of world religions, Cousins places him in the "vestige" tradition of trinitarian theology and comments that Panikkar has extended "this tradition into the sphere of mankind's religious experience as this has developed in its highest forms."[66]

As for some slight negative commentary, in 1979 Cousins wrote concerning Panikkar's Christology:

> . . . for some years now I have felt that Panikkar was not moving in
> the right direction. From my point of view, the crucial problem of an
> ecumenical Christology is precisely its particularity. . . . I thought
> that Panikkar should follow the same paradoxical strategy which he
> pursued in his Trinitarian theology - plunging into the very uniqueness
> of the Christian archetype, and discovering there, in its apparent

opposition to world religions, the very breakthrough that opens to the depth of their own archetypes.[67] . . . Much remains to be done in this area of Panikkar's Christology. I believe it is the linchpin of his emerging systematic theology; for it will fill out the necessary second pole of his theology to complement his Trinitarian theology, providing the focal point for drawing into the genre of systematic theology the many areas he has already developed in anthropology - for example, his notion of Theandrism - and in salvation history.[68]

A second author who evaluates Panikkar for the most part positively, but with some reservation, is M.M. Thomas. In 1970 in his "Foreword" to a work of Panikkar, Thomas predictably showers praise on the author for opening up "an inter-religious path which is different from both the intellectual exchange of religious ideas and a spiritual exchange involving an *epoche* [i.e., a bracketing] of faith."[69] Also, Panikkar is commended for reinterpreting "both the Hindu and the Christian doctrines in the process"[70] of developing his trinitarian theology.

Rather surprisingly for the author of a book's Foreword, Thomas permits himself a reservation in his assessment of Panikkar: "I am not sure whether this 'theandric synthesis' of various forms of spirituality does full justice to man's personal being in search of the plenitude of his personhood in society and history."[71]

A third author who likewise reacts very favourably to Panikkar but with less than complete enthusiasm is Kana Mitra, who sees Panikkar's concept of Trinity as undeveloped and only in its early stages.[72]

3. Critique of Continuity and Shifts in Panikkar's Trinitarian Thought

At the beginning of this chapter, a résumé was presented of the continuity and shifts in Panikkar's trinitarian theology. This section will offer a critique concerning the continuity and shifts. The critique will proceed in three subsections.

a) First Person of the Trinity

Panikkar's concept of the First Person of the Trinity remains constant throughout the development of his thought. The Father is always the inexpressible, that which gives everything to the Son. The Father can be known only through "Christ." Nothing can be said of the Father except through "Christ."

Since the publication of Panikkar's earliest trinitarian works much praise has been lavished on him for his treatment of the First Person of the Trinity. And rightly so. Panikkar not only has revived interest in the Church Fathers' position on the apophatic dimension of the Trinity but also has enriched traditional trinitarian theology by speaking of the Father in terms of the Nirvana experience of Buddhism. Panikkar's concept of the First Person of the Trinity has remained consistent, although there has been some attempt to explain further the meaning of the Nirvana experience[73] for the Western reader. It must be considered a flaw in Panikkar's treatment of the Father to have so emphasized the apophatic dimension of the Father as to rule out any expression in terms of Person or Creator.

b) Second Person of the Trinity

Panikkar's treatment of the Second Person of the Trinity is the most problematic. There is a sense in which his trinitarian theology can be reduced to his Christology because the First and Third Persons function in more hidden roles. This section will evaluate two shifts in Panikkar's treatment of the Second Person of the Trinity.

The first shift regards the fullness of revelation in Jesus Christ. In his earlier works Panikkar's concept of Christ is identified with Jesus of Nazareth. Panikkar sees the fullness of "Christ's" manifestation in Christianity, especially within the Roman Catholic Church. Non-Christians may have already experienced the same Christ in terms of Isvara, Buddha, etc.; but they lack contact with the fullness of Christ, available only in Christianity.

The later Panikkar seems to fear that to speak of the "fullness of revelation" in Jesus Christ would only obscure the more important point that he is trying to impress upon the Christian world. The Triune God has been revealed to Hindus and Buddhists long before Jesus. This revelation was not in terms of "traces"; it was as clear as in Christianity. Despite his praiseworthy intentions, Panikkar's interfaith concerns have led him to statements justifiably open to the charge of doctrinal exaggeration and "false irenicism."

There is a second shift in Panikkar's thinking regarding the Second Person of the Trinity. In 1991 Panikkar writes:

My book, *The Unknown Christ of Hinduism* (1964) was dedicated to the *Unknown Christ* as a parallel to Paul's "Unknown God" but was sometimes misunderstood to be speaking about the Christ known to christians and unknown to hindus, as I made clear in the 1980 [*sic*] edition. The "Unknown Christ of Hinduism" is *a fortiori* unknown to christians, and hindus do not need to call it by that name. They call 'it' by different names.[74]

How can Panikkar in 1964 entitle a work *The Unknown Christ of Hinduism* and then in 1991, commenting on the work, declare, "'The Unknown Christ of Hinduism' is *a fortiori* unknown to Christians, and hindus do not need to call it by that name."? The only plausible explanation seems to point to a shift in the meaning of the word Christ. In 1964 the word Christ is still being used in the traditional sense of the Christ of history. Therefore, "The Unknown Christ of Hinduism" is "the mystery of Jesus Christ that is present in a hidden way, perceptible to Christian faith alone, in the religious traditions, and Hinduism in particular."[75]

In the 1981 edition, as in Panikkar's subsequent writings, the meaning of the term Christ is expanded. Dupuis' summary[76] is useful:

> What, then, does Christ represent? Panikkar explains that, for him, Christ is the most powerful living symbol - but not one limited to the historical Jesus - of the fully human, divine, and cosmic reality that he calls the Mystery.[77] This symbol can have other names: for example, *Rama, Krishna, Ishvara, or Purusha.*[78] Christians call him "Christ," because it is in and through Jesus that they themselves have arrived at faith in the decisive reality. Each name, however, expresses the indivisible Mystery,[79] each being an unknown dimension of Christ.[80]

In summary, Panikkar's enigmatic words cited above certainly constitute a shift in his trinitarian and christological theology, even though he would deny it. This changed meaning given to the term Christ will be critiqued in the next chapter.

c) *Third Person of the Trinity*

With regard to the Third Person of the Trinity, the significant shift in Panikkar's later thought is, not in terms of who the Holy Spirit is, but rather in terms of where the Holy Spirit is found. In his earlier, more traditional thinking Panikkar recognizes the Holy Spirit to be present in a special way in the Christian Church. In his later works the Holy Spirit is no longer present in Christianity in any special way. The Holy Spirit is presented as dwelling at least equally beyond the Church and within every human person.

Shifting the emphasis on the presence of the Spirit from dwelling in a special way within the Christian Church to dwelling equally within every human person, even in the secular world, causes a few ecclesiological walls to begin to totter. Certain disturbing questions arise. Is there any reason for the existence of a Christian Church? Are the Sacraments, especially the Eucharist, of any special importance?

There is a way one could answer these questions superficially and inadequately by extrapolating from Panikkar's trinitarian theology as follows: the purpose of the Christian Church is to serve Christians; the Sacraments are important for Christians. Panikkar's claim that the Spirit is found expressed even more dynamically in the Advaita Vedanta and other Eastern traditions than in Christianity creates some wonderment, especially in the area of missiology.

Overall, Panikkar's Pneumatology poses some vexing problems. Nevertheless, his enhancement of the role of the Spirit, especially through the Advaita Vedanta tradition, opens up some exciting new vistas in a field of theology so undeveloped in the West.

4. Critique of Panikkar's Overall Proposal

Does Panikkar succeed in expanding and deepening the traditional concept of the Trinity in his attempt to bridge the gap between Christianity and Hinduism? Does he contribute in any way to trinitarian theology? What follows is an attempt to respond to these questions arising from Panikkar's overall proposal.

First, does Panikkar expand the traditional concept of the Trinity? Even in his earlier thought, expressed in *The Trinity and the Religious Experience of Man* (1973), he indeed expands the concept. He brings together within the Trinity the spiritualities of Hinduism and Buddhism. Also, he moves the notion of the Trinity beyond the traditional understanding towards one that exhibits more universal dimensions. Unfortunately, his trinitarian theology at this stage is seminal and underdeveloped, resembling more a cluster of spiritualities grouped under the umbrella of the Trinity rather than a holistic synthesis of the Trinity within the context of the world religions. Panikkar does indeed expand the traditional concept of the Trinity, but, more in terms of new ideas and new questions. Also he provides the opportunity for unprecedented constructive criticism in the area of world religions with the notion of the Triune God as the focus.

Secondly, does Panikkar deepen the concept of the Trinity? This question can be addressed from two viewpoints. From the first, Panikkar incorporates in his trinitarian theology such categories as Advaita from Hinduism and Nirvana from Buddhism. These categories theoretically involve depth-experience of the Triune God (or the Ultimate in Buddhism). Panikkar's choice of categories in which he attempts to situate his trinitarian theology is excellent. However, the depths of the concepts are never adequately made available to the Western reader.

From the other viewpoint, Panikkar presents a notion of Trinity centred within the human person. This he explores seminally in *The Unknown Christ of Hinduism*,[82] the main focus being the hidden "Christ" of Hinduism. Here again Panikkar is exploring the depth-experience of the Advaita tradition. It is evident that the theory he proposes indeed has the potential to deepen further the traditional concept of Trinity.

Thirdly, does Panikkar bridge the gap between Christianity and Hinduism? In his trinitarian thought from the earliest stages, Panikkar really sees no gap in need of bridging between the two religions. The gap that he seeks to bridge is more in terms of dialogue, communication, awareness and experience. The gap exists between the adherents of the particular religions in their awareness and experience of the "Trinity."

Fourthly, does Panikkar contribute in any way to Christian trinitarian theology? Certainly he does. However, he does so at the cost of the "Christianness" of the Trinity. His trinitarian concept has opened new horizons and plumbed new depths in which Christians can speak of the Trinity outside of traditional parameters. However, in viewing his final position on the Trinity, it is evident that the Blessed Trinity of traditional Christianity can no longer be fully identified with Panikkar's Trinity. This does not mean that his notion of Trinity is totally invalid. Panikkar's Trinity expresses truth about the Godhead in the world religions and in the "sacred experience" of the secular world. This is not in real opposition to traditional Christian thought that proclaims loudly the universality of the Triune God. Where his thought falters is in the place given to the historical Jesus. Exalting the various expressions (Isvara, Buddha, Krishna) and experiences of God to such unprecedented heights and with such impact is one of the great contributions of Professor Panikkar. However, traditional trinitarian theology cannot remain intact if not grounded firmly in the Christ Event. Panikkar's claims to the contrary notwithstanding, this groundedness is not clearly evident in his works.

Notes

1   Panikkar, *Unknown Christ of Hinduism* (1964), ix.
2   *Ibid.*
3   *Ibid.* (1964), 26; (1981), 60.
4   *Ibid.* (1964), 131.
5   *Ibid.* (1981), 161.
6   *Ibid.* (1964), 131.
7   *Ibid.* (1981), 162.
8   *Ibid.* (1964), 124.
9   *Ibid.* (1981), 154.
10 See *ibid.* (1964), 126, 128; (1981), 156.
11 Panikkar, *Unknown Christ of Hinduism* (1964), ix, *passim.*
12 Ibid., 17.
13 *Ibid.*, 59-60.
14 *Ibid.*, 17.
15 *Ibid.*, (1981), 49.
16 *Ibid.* (1964), 26.
17 *Ibid.* (1981), 60.
18 *Ibid.* (1964), 21. Also see *ibid.*, 60.
19 See *ibid.* (1964), 26; (1981), 59.
20 *Ibid.* (1964), 26; (1981), 60.
21 *Ibid.* (1964), 26.
22 *Ibid.* (1981), 60.
23 *Ibid.* (1964), 60.
24 *Ibid.* (1981), 93
26 See Panikkar, "Monotheism," in *Gifford Lectures*, No. 1.
27 Most recently Panikkar is more tolerant of monotheism.
28 Written about ten years prior to publication
31 Panikkar, "Instead of a Foreword: An Open Letter," xiii.
32 Macquarrie, *Principles of Christian Theology*, 7
33 *Dei Verbum*, art.2.
34 Macquarrie, *Principles of Christian Theology*, 11.
35 See Raimundo Panikkar, *The Silence of God. The Answer of the Buddha* (Maryknoll: Orbis Books, 1989). See, for example, 141.
36 See Cousins, "Raimundo Panikkar and the Christian Systematic Theology of the Future," 148.
37 See Panikkar, *Unknown Christ of Hinduism* (1964), 120-21.
39 Cousins, "Raimundo Panikkar and the Christian Systematic Theology of the Future," 153.
43 See Panikkar, "The Radical Trinity," in *Gifford Lectures*, No. 6.
45 See Panikkar, *Worship and Secular Man* and *The Vedic Experience*.

46 Walter Strolz, "Panikkar's Encounter with Hinduism," in *Dialogue and Syncretism*, ed. Jerald Gort, Hendrik Vroom, Rein Fernhout, and Anton Wessels (Grand Rapids: William B. Eerdmans, 1988), 149.

47 Odette Baumer-Despeigne, "A Pilgrimage to One's Own Roots - A Precondition to Religious Dialogue?" in *Interreligious Dialogue: Voices from a New Frontier*, 77.

48 Nalini Devdas, "The Theandrism of Raimundo Panikkar and Trinitarian Parallels in Modern Hindu Thought," *Journal of Ecumenical Studies* 17 (1980): 617.

49 Anthony Kelly, *The Trinity of Love: A Theology of the Christian God* (Michael Glazier: Delaware, 1989), 236.

50 *Ibid.*, 243.

51 See James Kodera, "Beyond Agreeing to Disagree - A Future Direction in Interfaith Dialogue," in *Interreligious Dialogue: Voices from a New Frontier*, 158.

52 Rowan Williams, "Trinity and Pluralism," in *Christian Uniqueness Reconsidered. The Myth of a Pluralistic Theology of Religions*, ed. Gavin D'Costa (Orbis: Maryknoll, 1990), 11.

53 *Ibid.*, 14.

54 Knitter, *No Other Name*, 153.

55 Paul Knitter, "The Wider Ecumenism: Exploring New Directions," *Ecumenical Trends* 15 (1986): 135.

56 Gavin D'Costa, "Christ, the Trinity and Religious Plurality," in *Christian Uniqueness Reconsidered. The Myth of a Pluralistic Theology of Religions*, 16.

57 See Claude Geffré, "La foi à l'âge du pluralisme religieux,"*La vie spirituelle* 143 (1989): 805-815.

58 *Ibid.*, 810.

59 Jacques Dupuis, *Jesus Christ at the Encounter of World Religions*, trans. Robert R. Barr (Maryknoll: Orbis Books, 1991), 184-188.

60 *Ibid.*, 184.

61 *Ibid.*, 187. Whether Panikkar indeed is guilty of so blatantly departing from Christological orthodoxy is questionable.

62 Dupuis, *Jesus Christ at the Encounter of World Religions*, 188. Also see Robert Smet, *Essai sur la pensée de Raimundo Panikkar: Une contribution indienne à la théologie des religions et à la christologie* (Louvain-La Neuve: Centre d'histoire des religions, 1981), 46-47. It must be pointed out that nowhere does Panikkar state that the "*Logos* acts elsewhere in identical fashion." What emerges here is the complexity of the issue. It is complex because of the problem of language and translation. The problem occurs in crossing over to other religious traditions with a particular concept in mind; the difficulty arises in reading an author from a horizontal perspective, where experiencing Christ in Christianity cannot be read with the same methods of interpretation as experiencing "Christ" in Advaita or "Christ" in Buddhism.

63 See Ewert Cousins, "The Trinity and World Religions." *Journal of Ecumenical Studies* 7 (1970): 476-498.

64 See Cousins, "Raimundo Panikkar and the Christian Systematic Theology of the Future," 148.

65 *Ibid.*

66 *Ibid.*

67 At this point Cousins adds parenthetically, "A year ago at the Castelli Conference in Rome, . . . I detected that he had done just that, although the position . . . was very much submerged in the text and has not to this day been formulated by Panikkar in print." *Ibid.*, 149.

68 *Ibid.*, 149-150.

69 M.M. Thomas, "Foreword," to Panikkar's *The Trinity and World Religions*, vii.

70 *Ibid.*

71 *Ibid.*, viii.

72 See Kana Mitra, *Catholic-Hinduism: Vedantic Investigation of Raimundo Panikkar's Attempt at Bridgebuilding* (New York: University Press of America, 1987), 131. Mitra is a Hindu scholar engaged in Catholic-Hindu dialogue.

73 See Panikkar, *The Silence of God*, 37-52.

74 Panikkar, "Christophany for Our Times," 11.

75 This is Dupuis' summary of Panikkar's use of the term Christ in the 1964 edition. Dupuis, *Jesus Christ at the Encounter of World Religions*, 184-185.

76 See Dupuis, *Jesus Christ at the Encounter of World Religions*, 185-186.

77 See Panikkar, *Unknown Christ of Hinduism* (1981), 23, 26-27.

78 see *ibid.*, 27.

79 See *ibid.*, 29.

80 See *ibid.*, 30.

82 Especially in the second edition (1981).

Chapter V

Further Problems Deriving from Panikkar's Concept of Trinity

In examining Panikkar's trinitarian thought as it has developed over the years, several questions arise. First is the issue of history. Does Panikkar take it seriously? Because he is wrestling with experiential systems, especially the Advaita Vedanta system and the term cosmotheandrism, the concept of history shifts from a Western to an Eastern understanding. Since this shift is not always explicit, Panikkar is often misunderstood. For example, when he speaks of the various Hindu Gods as being equal to Christ, the immediate reaction is to critique these Gods from the viewpoint of Western historical categories. However, these categories are very different from the Eastern religious perspective which places subjective meditational experiences within "historical" categories.

The second question concerns Christianity itself. Is it taken seriously? Again, this question is addressed because Panikkar is developing his trinitarian theology out of vastly different religious systems, including Christianity. He certainly takes the Lord Krishna in Hinduism seriously, even to the extent of claiming Krishna to be "equal" to Christ. Consequently, it is valid to question whether Christianity is indeed being taken seriously.

The third question is that of the Christ Event. Is the historical Jesus unique? Does Panikkar really accord the Christ Event sufficient prominence? It is the question that emerges for the reader at every stage of Panikkar's trinitarian thought. The Christ Event is the anchor which grounds Christianity as a historical religion immersed within the mystery of the Blessed Trinity.

The following sections of this chapter will pursue these three questions. In addition, two other questions will be addressed. First, is Panikkar advocating a new ecumenical religion in light of his dialogue with the world religions, and secondly, what is the effect of his trinitarian concept on traditional understandings of missiology?

A. Is History Taken Seriously?

The trinitarian theology of Panikkar has aroused considerable controversy. Among the suspect elements in his thought is the question of history. Is it taken seriously? Is there a Western way of thinking about history based on chronological events that is radically different from the Eastern mentality? Two thousand years of Christian history represent a certain mindset. Is it possible to look at the Eastern religions, especially Hinduism and Buddhism, and speak of events and their content with a Western sense of history; or is it necessary to broaden the parameters of the concept of history or even view history as myth in order to deal authentically with religious experiential systems, such as many of the schools of Hinduism and Buddhism?

Central to the entire question of history is the understanding and interpretation of experience over the centuries, especially when encased in layers of cultural sediment. Bernard Lonergan states:

> In brief, the historical process itself and, within it, the personal development of the historian give rise to a series of different standpoints. The different standpoints give rise to different selective processes. The different selective processes give rise to different histories that are (1) not contradictory, (2) not complete information and not complete explanation, but (3) incomplete and approximate portrayals of an enormously complex reality.[1]

The question of history has been problematic for centuries. Historians have wrestled with this issue and have challenged many past interpretations that had resulted in a stagnant and limited idea of history.

Kaufman points out that all historical knowledge is "relational" in character: "There is no such thing as a historical object-in-itself; there is only the object-in-relation-to-the-historian (as mediated through 'historical evidence'), and it is this object alone that the historian can reconstruct."[2] Carr states, "the facts of history never come to us 'pure,' since they do not and cannot exist in a pure form: they are always refracted through the mind of the recorder."[3]   The task of interpreting history is indeed complex.

What Panikkar attempts to deal with as he develops his trinitarian theology is a "total history," which for him includes the collapse of history,[4] in his crossing over to the world religions in order to penetrate their depth of experience. However, the question remains. Has he taken history seriously, especially as it relates to Christian history.

This section will first examine Panikkar's understanding of history and then invoke some guidelines that stipulate the tasks of the Christian historian. It will conclude by briefly assessing whether Panikkar has adequately fulfilled the guidelines of a Christian historian.

Panikkar's concept of history is based on three different modes of consciousness. He sees human memory as extending to roughly 6,500 years. He states that presently we are at the end of the historical period. He claims, "we are at the end not only of *a* historical period, but of *the* historical period of mankind, which is to say that we are witnessing the collapse of the myth of history."[5]

The three kairological moments of human consciousness that he proposes are based on his "diachronical and diatopical experience of cultures and peoples."[6]   The prehistorical period of consciousness dates from the prehistoric person to the period of the written word. Religious writings mark the beginning of the historical period. The posthistorical period begins with the discovery of the power of the atom. According to Panikkar the splitting of the atom has exploded historical consciousness, thus marking the end of what is commonly viewed as history.[7]

In considering whether Panikkar has taken history seriously, it is useful to examine the work of the Christian historian. As one historian puts it, the task of the Christian historian is "to achieve a synthesis between the facts of history and his Christian beliefs. He must be objective in regard to the facts, but at the same time, he must face the challenge of Christ."[8]   Donald Masters employs several criteria to determine whether the Christian historian has performed his task well. The first criterion requires the historian to be rigorous and unbiased in stating the facts of history. The historian should also be "scientific in the use of orderly techniques for discovering and classifying the factual material of history."[9]

If one thing can be said about Raimon Panikkar with regard to stating the facts of history, it is that he is certainly inclusive. The facts of history that he takes great pains to explain involve not only Christian history but also the history of other cultures. Some of the misunderstanding arises from crossing over from a historical interpretation based on a given culture to an interpretation based on another culture where the tools of exegesis are so different. One example would be the creation hymn, "The Unknown God, the Golden Embryo."[10] This account of creation would have to be interpreted within its own Eastern context. Another instance of stating the facts of history from an Eastern mindset is the reference made to Gaudapada in a commentary. Gaudapada is cited as one of the first historic philosophers of Vedanta and one of the first expounders of its non-dualistic aspect. "There is a tradition that Sankara, who lived in the seventh century A.D., met Gaudapada and received his blessing."[11] Scholars agree that Sankara's meeting with Gaudapada is true, "but that they met each other on the yogic plane, where, the spiritual eye of the aspirant being opened, a direct communion with the great souls of the past may be obtained."[12]

The purely Western and often Christian approach moves in the direction of given facts, interpreted by modern scholarship and technology, in such areas as archaeology, anthropology and historiography. The historical process from ancient to modern times is quite complex and is further complicated by the fact that "modern philosophy of history - on a Christian basis - and modern historical methods - on a classical basis - have never quite agreed with each other."[13]

Panikkar is much more fluid than both Eastern and Western historians and indeed unique in his interpretation of history. He is faced with the immense difficulty of dealing with religious experience stemming from vastly different approaches to the meaning of history. He is confronted both by historical events based on Western categories and by "historical mythological experiential events" based on Eastern categories. This is further complicated by the observation Lane makes that there are no uninterpreted events in history, because essentially the person who selects interprets.[14]

It appears that Panikkar has tried to deal adequately with history. He has certainly dealt adequately with history from the Eastern viewpoint, which does not attach as much importance to specific historical events as does the West. However, in the process of doing so it appears that he has toned down the importance of the Christ Event historically.

The second criterion proposed by Donald Masters is that the Christian historian should "have a special regard for truth."[15] The depth at which Panikkar searches for truth from the perspective of the experience of the human person is without parallel. It is difficult to ascertain the many intricacies involved in such a task. Nevertheless, some observations are in order. Panikkar is not satisfied with being an outside observer who extrapolates from his experience and knowledge of concrete facts. He goes beyond and probes into what is happening within the individual. He seeks to view things from the "inner vision" of the person, beyond the confines of history taken in a narrow sense.

For instance, Panikkar is concerned more with how people experience themselves and their God than with the more Christian Western notion of God as experienced through the person of Jesus, who lived two thousand years ago and started his ministry at about thirty years of age, in a certain land, etc. The truth of Jesus as the Christ is not an issue with Panikkar or perhaps more accurately with the "later" Panikkar.

From the perspective of Christianity, Panikkar is concerned with the question: How is the Risen Christ experienced? But even more so, is he concerned from the perspective of Eastern thought with the question: How are the Gods experienced[16] and what is the experience of non-duality in which Atman equals Brahman in relation to the Trinity?

Panikkar explores truth from numerous sources. He draws on scientific data and philosophies of ancient and modern times, both from the East and the West. He employs the tools of chemistry and physics. He taps into cultural data from Hindus, Buddhists, tribal religions, Christianity and modern non-religious cultures, always careful to point out the complexities within any given system. For example, he attempts to see through the lenses of the interior of Hinduism. He states, "The self-understanding of Hinduism emanates from entirely different premises than that of Christianity: they cannot be simplistically compared."[17] Hinduism "does not possess, strictly speaking, very much historical awareness."[18] Panikkar is able to draw parallels, develop, and even synthesize theories, although in the past these have appeared to be in diametrical opposition. The influence of mathematics[19] and geometry[20] is evident in his writing as he rigorously searches for truth and explanations still foreign to the Western Christian mind.

The third criterion established by Donald Masters is that the "Christian historian will apply Christian standards in the evaluation of human conduct."[21] Masters expands this statement to include the Christian historian being able to "evaluate human conduct" in the light of the cleavage between good and evil. The historian also must try to remain objective in the task of probing human behaviour amid all its varieties.[22]

To begin to understand Raimon Panikkar, it is important to realize that the terms "Christian historian" and "Christian standards" must take on different nuances. Panikkar would certainly consider himself "Christian." He is an active Roman Catholic Priest. At the same time, however, Panikkar has gradually seen himself as one who can easily be called Buddhist or Hindu or Moslem[23] in the sense that the trinitarian God expresses the truth of cosmotheandric intuition in all of these religions and even outside the parameters of organized religion. Panikkar focuses on many systems, yet he is also a Christian dealing with history.

This also affects the meaning of the term "Christian standards." In Panikkar's system "Christian standards" are in no way superior to "Hindu standards" or "Buddhist standards" when the question of good and evil is taken into account. Panikkar would oppose strongly any religion, even Christianity, if it gave the impression that it held the supreme measuring apparatus for good and evil in the world. He would seem to differ from Pope John Paul II:

> As the third Millennium of the Redemption draws near, God is preparing a great springtime for Christiantity, and we can already see its first signs. In fact, both in the non-Christian world and in the traditionally Christian world, people are gradually drawing closer to Gospel ideals and values.[24]

While wearing Christian spectacles, it is often difficult to look at people in other religions and realize that many of their values and ideals stem from their own religious systems and often have nothing to do with the Christian Gospel as such. To speak to the Buddhist of non-violence as a uniquely Christian virtue would be absurd. Also, Buddha preached about the equality of women and men five hundred years before Jesus, although Buddha had difficulty practicing that ideal in his own life. The origins of good and evil in the different religious systems emerge from very diverse sources and are understood very differently as one moves from one religion to the next.[25]

Because of Panikkar's immersion in Eastern cultures and religions, he is able to "evaluate human conduct" not only according to Christian standards but also according to the standards of Eastern cultures and religions. Also, it is interesting to note that the concept of good and evil in Eastern religions is closely linked with the understanding of the various Gods[26] and the spiritual growth of persons through self-awareness in a way that is foreign to the Western Christian world.

The question of variety and universality[27] is one to which Panikkar has devoted much time and effort. He has probed, not just as an objective observer, but also as one who sees from within, not just from the outside but also experientially. It appears that he has fulfilled another criterion in considering the task and responsibility of the Christian historian, albeit with slight nuances affecting the meaning of the word "Christian" and the way "good and evil" are examined.

A fourth criterion offered by Donald Masters is that the "Christian historian will see the events of history within the framework of the eschatological events in which he believes."[28] Masters also asserts how important it is for the historian to be cautious in his attempt to explain "how the events of history specifically manifest the working out of God's purpose."[29]

Panikkar's vision of the events of history and their relationship to the *eschaton* is clearly different from that of the traditional Christian interpretation.[30] His understanding of the suffering people of the world is also linked with his understanding of eschatology. He sees most of humanity living and suffering in subhuman conditions in which theism and monotheism cease to be relevant.[31] A root problem in Panikkar's writings is the concept of theism,[32] and especially of monotheism. This affects drastically the understanding of the Christ Event as well as of the entire area of eschatology. In Panikkar's earlier thought Jesus holds a supreme position; however, in Panikkar's recent thinking, as expressed in the *Gifford Lectures*, there is very little mention of Jesus. This de-emphasis on Jesus is partly defensible on the basis of the title of the lectures: "Trinity and Atheism." Panikkar definitely does not fulfill the present criterion, if the events of history are to be seen from a Western Christian perspective of eschatology. There is no doubt that he believes in the unfolding of God's purpose through history and beyond; but because Panikkar's notion of God is nuanced, it no longer fits into the framework of what is commonly understood as eschatology. Panikkar, of course, would not mean that Christians should not explore new approaches in seeing how "God's" purpose unfolds in the events of history.

Masters' fifth criterion is that history from the viewpoint of the Christian historian should also recognize "the gospel's ability to transform lives."[33] Panikkar's idea of the Good News includes not only the Gospel but also the Vedas and the Upanishads, the Koran and the Tipitaka, as well as all the other treasured scriptures of the world.[34] In fact, Panikkar's perception of the Good News would go beyond the religious systems and their contents to such elements as the "stone" to bring about a realization of the Good News of God.

According to Masters' sixth and final criterion the Christian historian acknowledges a God who fulfills his promises and who is faithful to his people, that is, "to Abraham, to Moses, to Gideon, to David, to St. Paul, to Luther, and to many others."[35] The Christian sees hope for the world in Christ. Masters quotes the hymn "On Christ the solid rock I stand, all other ground is sinking sand."[36]

Because Panikkar's understanding of God is neither monotheistic nor trinitarian in the traditional sense, his continuing claims to reflect Christian orthodoxy fall short of full credence. Christ, "the solid rock," the Saviour, is no longer seen as identified solely with Jesus. "All other ground" is viewed, not as sinking sand, but, as permeated by the cosmotheandric reality as a fertile field for historical progression and transhistorical consciousness incarnated in the world.

In conclusion, Panikkar does take history very seriously. However, in the development of his trinitarian theology, history as it relates to Christianity, especially to the Christ Event, takes a crashing fall. The earlier Panikkar tries to deal with the difficulties posed by history as he moves from Christianity to the experiental Eastern religions. The later Panikkar, however, comes down heavily on the side of the limitations of history, even suggesting that the Christian linear way of viewing history must collapse in order to open the door to a recognition of the true universality of the Blessed Trinity. Panikkar maintains that it is imperative that the present mould in which the traditional Christian concept of the Trinity is trapped must be broken, in order that the Trinity may be recognized in religions where history, along with time and space, assumes a secondary role.

B. Is Christianity Taken Seriously?

Because of the radical nature of Panikkar's trinitarian thought, which draws heavily on the religious experience of other religions and is anchored in the numerous Eastern religious myths and scriptural discourses of non-Christian religions, it is valid to ask whether Christianity is taken seriously in his thinking.

This section will consist of two parts. First, Panikkar's changing notion of Christianity will be briefly considered. The second part will

address the question: In his attempt to universalize the trinitarian concept
has he failed to take Christianity seriously?

Panikkar's image of Christianity has undergone radical change during
the last thirty years. His *The Trinity and Religious Experience of Man*
(1973), although daring in its attempt to make connections with the
Advaita Vedanta experience in Hinduism and the Nirvana experience of
Buddhism, still retains a sense of the Trinity in keeping with traditional
Christian interpretation.

In reading this work one is impressed with a devout Roman Catholic
in touch with deep spiritual experiences of both Hinduism and Buddhism
and trying to understand and express these realities in the context of a
universal Triune God affirmed by Christianity. Even in his earliest
writings, Panikkar reflects his identity as a Roman Catholic grasping
and expressing the authentic nature of the Advaita (non-dualistic)
experience and that of Nirvana (blowing-out, enlightenment, God is neti,
neti: not this, not that) and linking these experiences with the Triune
God.

Few Roman Catholics have ever arrived at this insight and awareness
with such clear understanding of the world religions; and fewer yet Roman
Catholic priests have been so bold, daring and thorough in their search
and expression as to make such connections with other cultures, as they
express their experience and relationship with God. Even with the novelty
of his thought, Panikkar at this stage still retains what reflects a Christian
theology as he speaks of the Triune God permeating the diverse religious
experiences of all nations. Because Panikkar is making connections with
major religious traditions, his trinitarian framework has a universal
dimension; at the same time it remains clearly Christian.

In one of his earliest works, the first edition (1964) of his classic
The Unknown Christ of Hinduism, Panikkar is still speaking of Jesus
Christ as the fullness of God's revelation. Although Isvara is seen as the
Christ in Hinduism even then, there is still a traditional strain in Panikkar's
thinking. He views Trinity within Christianity as the reality that embraces
all religious experiences. Discussing the question of salvation Panikkar
remarks, "The ultimate reason for this universal idea of Christianity, an
idea which makes possible the Catholic embrace of every people and
religion, lies in the Christian conception of Christ not *only* as the historical
redeemer, but *also* as the unique Son of God, as the Second Person of the
Trinity, as the only one ontological-temporal and eternal-link between
God and the world."[39] Panikkar attempts a penetration of the Advaita
system to formulate what he terms "The Hindu Trinity".[40] Nevertheless,

the heart or core of his theology remains within the context of Christianity, although his extrapolation in terms of a universal Christianity moves him deep into the religious experiences of the Advaita Vedanta system.

One of the primary shifts in Raimon Panikkar's thought occurs in the revised edition of his *The Unknown Christ of Hinduism* (1981). Although previously he held to the Trinity as an overarching framework linking the religious experiences of Christians and other traditions, now the experience of the Trinity is seen as being able to be encountered without ever interacting with Christianity or even with Jesus. Jesus becomes not the Christ but a Christ among many Christs, with Isvara being the active presence or concept in the mind of the Advaitin seeking the non-dualistic encounter with or awareness of Brahman.

Panikkar's thinking shifts to numerous systems of thought and their search for a relationship with God. Panikkar is convinced that their religious systems experience genuine contact and indeed "incarnation" of God in their midst. This is conveyed in their own symbols, myths, languages and rituals. Even at this point Panikkar would maintain that he is still functioning within Christianity which believes in a Triune God who is universal and present especially within religious systems. In his trinitarian theology Panikkar has moved internally into the deepest regions of the various religious systems to experience the Triune God. He discovers God within these religions, but is it the Triune God of Christianity?

Not all would agree that Panikkar has found the Christian Triune God in the world's religions. His thinking is even more problematic when one realizes that he is referring not only to religions but even to atheism or any system of thought in which the human person is seeking something deeper in life.

Panikkar later reaches a new stage of synthesis in his understanding of Christianity. He emerges with the insight that a new consciousness has to be achieved in Christianity in order to arrive at a genuine integration of reality. In a pointed article he proposes an understanding of the cosmotheandric intuition as vital to all religions, if one is to come to terms with reality as expressed throughout the universe.[42]

Although Panikkar is constantly using Christian images and examples to describe his position, there is a sense that he is no longer speaking about Christianity or Catholicism but rather is developing a world religion that barely resembles Christianity.[43] He certainly continues to adhere to Christianity. He would claim that it depends on how Christianity is defined. Panikkar does not accept a traditional, and for him, narrow description of Christianity. He is looking for both new wine skins and new wine. For example, this is evident in his use of the Transfiguration as a symbol of his study of reality which leads to the notion of the cosmotheandric vision:

> The mystery of the Transfiguration could stand as the symbol of this study. Nothing is despised, nothing left over. Everything is integrated, assumed, transfigured. Nothing is postponed into the future: the whole presence is here. Nothing is put aside as non-redeemable: the entire body as well as past history is integrated. Transfiguration is not a hallucination of some nicer reality or an escapism into a higher plane. It is the total integrated vision of the seamless garment of the total reality: the cosmotheandric vision.[44]

The *Gifford Lectures,* delivered by Panikkar in 1989, typify a new stage in his concept of Christianity. Although the series is entitled "Trinity and Atheism," one is surprised at the scant mention of Trinity in a traditional Christian sense. His lecture, "Inadequacy of All Theisms," deals primarily with his almost violent opposition to monotheism. His arrival at an understanding of Christianity no longer monotheistic, even if expressed in terms of a Triune God, would seem to indicate that Panikkar's image of Christianity loses much of Christian orthodoxy.

After the examination of Panikkar's changing notion of Christianity, a response will be given to the question: In his attempt to universalize the trinitarian concept, has he failed to take Christianity seriously? In wrestling with the complexities of Christianity and the religious experience of the world religions, Panikkar has no doubt taken Christianity very, very seriously. However, his spiritual and intellectual growth has opened up for him new vistas of religious experience with its many diverse expressions.

Although earlier in his life as a young professor, Panikkar had been more in touch with abstract religious thought, return to his Indian roots brought him into contact with other new experiences, both religious and secular. He was plunged by birth into two diverse religions, drawn to the priesthood as a Roman Catholic presbyter and swept into currents placing him at the pulse of society and the tensions of life. Exposure to a wide range of diverse religious thinking through personal experience, interpersonal and intrapersonal dialogue, along with constant exchange with the secular world has left him in a unique position.

Panikkar saw his understanding of Christianity as a process of natural evolution. He felt that it was impossible to retain old modes of thinking when he personally sensed a burst of new religious awareness, extending to all peoples and all of creation.

Being an intellectual, and an original thinker, as well as striving towards mysticism, Panikkar felt the need to tread on new ground. At times it might appear that this treading is rather trespassing on the grounds of others at the expense of abandoning one's own premises. And yet, others may see him as a prophet. Whatever the case, it seems that if Panikkar felt compelled by conscience, and moved by the Spirit, to pronounce what he considered a truth previously unheard by Christians, then he simply had very little choice but to move towards his modified concept of Trinity, his new Christology and later what he termed a more mature version of the cosmotheandric vision.

It is not apparent why Panikkar has moved so far away from the person of Jesus, the foundation of Christianity. Although Panikkar has sometimes been called a mystic, it appears as if his faith-experience of the person and presence of Jesus is lacking in its Christian uniqueness. Whenever Panikkar speaks about the Christian's experiencing the presence of Jesus, he is quick to make the link with the Advaitin experience of Isvara or the Krishnaite experiencing Krishna, as well as other similar connections. Panikkar grapples with the question of what it means to be an authentic Christian. He realizes that living the Christian message in "depth and plenitude" means also discovering and appreciating the wealth of religious experience in other religions.[46]

In assessing whether Panikkar has failed to take Christianity seriously in his attempt to universalize the trinitarian concept, it appears that he has tried to be faithful to Christianity. However, his later trinitarian notion, his Christology and his understanding of history have resulted in the undermining of certain foundational layers of Christianity. To be sure, Panikkar has tried to take Christianity seriously; however, in the process of trying to take equally seriously Hinduism and Buddhism, as well as other religious experiences, Christianity has suffered immensely. Panikkar has in effect rejected some of the foundational tenets of Christianity.

C. Is the Historical Jesus Unique?

This section will examine the Christ Event and consider whether Panikkar's decision to seemingly bypass it is a valid one in the context of the Eastern religious systems.[47] The Christ Event has always been for Panikkar a significant and urgent question, as reflected throughout his writings dating from the early sixties to the present.[48] His primary concern has been that the universality of "Christ" is at stake in the confrontation between Christianity and the world religions.[49] Panikkar's objective is to present "Christ" to the world in an authentic universal manner that takes into serious account the religious experiences of the various religions. Others have taken seriously the religious experiences of other religions.[50] Panikkar, however, goes a step further. Even in the sixties, he recognizes the validity of the experience of the Godhead within other religions, without their having to enter into the religious experience of Christianity, that is, having to come into contact with the name of Jesus. Panikkar's struggle with the Hindu Trinity in the early sixties[51] indicates how deeply situated he is in this stream of thought that will permeate his works for almost another three decades. In the 1960's Panikkar sees himself "as a man impelled by a living faith in Christ"[52] and committed to "The essential reality of a true, historical and sacramental Christ."[53]

What is critical here is belief in the birth, death and resurrection of Jesus Christ, who is the only Son of God. The Church's position goes back to the very beginning of her history. This traditional Christian belief is summarized by Pope John Paul II's Encyclical Letter, *Redemptoris Missio*, as follows: "Christ is the one Saviour of all, the only one able to reveal God and lead to God."[54] This statement, according to the Holy Father, finds its foundation in the words of Peter:

> . . . this man is standing before you in good health by the name of Jesus of Nazareth whom you crucified, whom God raised from the dead. . . . There is salvation in no one else, for there is no other name under heaven given among mortals by which we must be saved.[55]

The Pope contends that the statement of Peter has universal value for all peoples, and he emphasizes that salvation can come only from Jesus Christ.[56] Panikkar in his exploration of the question "who is Jesus" points to Peter's reply "You are the Messiah, the Son of the Living God."[57] Panikkar argues that this statement was not meant for the Hindu, who was not expecting a Messiah.[58] Also, in Hinduism the concept of son of God is common in the sense that we are all sons and daughters of God. Therefore, in Hinduism the statement that Jesus is the Son of the living God would be easily accepted, but with a different meaning.

Panikkar's earlier thought reflects a sense of the Christ Event as integral to his faith stance, while at the same time he feels free to reach out to adherents of other religious traditions and affirm them in their practices and beliefs as authentic followers of the one true God. This God can be Brahman, Allah or even a reality within the concept or experience of Nirvana, where God cannot be described: God is *neti, neti* (not this, not that). In Panikkar's Christology Buddha, Krishna, Siva, Isvara or Bhagavan can be the living Christ.[59] Elsewhere Panikkar makes the same point: Christ who is "present, active, unknown and hidden may be called Isvara, Bhagavan, or even 'Krsna,' 'Narayana' or 'Siva.'"[60] Panikkar sees Christ active in all religions. Panikkar is often cited as holding that there are many Christs, which admittedly he does assert clearly in his *The Unknown Christ of Hinduism*. However, what he means is that there are many expressions or homeomorphic equivalents of the one Christ in the world religions. Panikkar states that there are not two or more Christs. Christ is "all in all."[61] Panikkar's position seems to contradict the traditional stance of the Catholic Church.

One statement of the Pope would be very difficult to reconcile with Panikkar's thought: "Although participated forms of mediation of different kinds and degrees are not excluded, they acquire meaning and value *only* from Christ's own mediation, and they cannot be understood as parallel or complementary to his."[62]

Theologians have wrestled with the inadequacy of all "names" for God, especially the neo-Platonic mystical theologians who have favored the apophatic approaches of God. However, a certain groundedness needs to be present. That is, "(1) Christ as Logos, as the Image of God, the Second 'Person' of the Trinity, and (2) the Christian spiritual experience of love in the Christ as an experience of God's own self as Spirit - the Spirit who, as God, lovingly unites us to Father and Son even as the Spirit unites Father and Son to one another in God."[63] It is this groundedness in Jesus Christ that Panikkar lacks, although he would claim that his theory is consistent with and foundational to a universal application of Christ as Saviour of all humanity.

Panikkar contends that "Christianity's claim to have seen Christ as the Pantocrator, by whom and for whom everything has been made, Alpha and Omega, beginning and end of the universe, First Born of creation, universal Redeemer and only Saviour, still holds true. But the proper *context* of these affirmations must be investigated."[64] It appears, however, that it is more than the context that troubles Panikkar.

His assertion that there are many Christs calls into question Jesus as the foundation of Christianity. In the later edition of *The Unknown Christ of Hinduism* (1981) and in the *Gifford Lectures* (1989), the link between

Christ and Jesus appears to be completely severed.[65] After subtle shifts in Panikkar's thinking, Jesus as symbol of Christ in Christianity is no longer the saving presence for all of humanity. For Panikkar there are many Saviours. The Second Person of the Trinity is the Christ, but many Saviours perform the function of Christ or are "equal" to Christ. These many expressions of the one Christ are responsible for raising up humans as sons and daughters to the Father, with the effect of non-duality between humans and the Deity being brought about by the Holy Spirit.

The greatest rupture with traditional Christian thought occurs with Panikkar's shift from the Christ Event as the focus of trinitarian understanding. This shift emerges in the process of rethinking traditional trinitarian theology in order to reflect the authentic religious experiences of adherents of other religious systems.

Again, Panikkar does not intend explicitly to reject the Christ Event as understood by Christians; he is concerned with breaking new ground in the probing of the Godhead in order to include others as part of that magnificent church that he termed the catholic church, the universal church. In the process of moving towards adherents of other religious systems, not abstractly through an exchange of ideas on the rational level, but through intrareligious dialogue deep within his own being, Panikkar shifts from the Christ Event as the focus of the trinitarian understanding. The shift involves a movement towards a trinitarian theology that barely resembles traditional Christian faith.

The primary accusation leveled at Panikkar by theologians is that he undermines the importance of the Christian mystery[66] and the universality of the Christ Event, taken in the traditional sense. Panikkar replies in one of the most recent defenses of his perceived position:

> It seems that I am thrown into the same bag with all those who defend a certain eclecticism and undermine the centrality of the Christian mystery, as if I were espousing relativism, when - in fact - I am propounding relativity. The pluralism I defend is in no way a negation of the centrality of Christ when we speak Christian language, or when we think and write about the Christian economy of salvation. All that Christian orthodoxy affirms is right: Christ is divine. What Christianity denies may be wrong without impinging upon orthodoxy.
>
> Christ is what orthodox Christians affirm. But Christians have no exclusive jurisdiction over Christ; they do not have an exhaustive knowledge of Christ. They cannot deny other possible aspects of that Mystery that they call Christ.[67]

In an even more recent article, Pannikkar again defends himself against the accusation[68] that he does not take the historical Jesus seriously:

> I do not think it is the case. I may say only this. The historical Jesus is paramount for the Christian. The Christian believes in, finds, discovers, Christ *in* and *through* Jesus, the son of Mary. Were it not for Jesus, the Christian would not have the revelation or not discover the Mystery, hidden before all eons in the womb of reality. And in Christ are enclosed all the riches of Divinity and Humanity.[69]

For Panikkar Christ is trans-historic as well as historic.[70] He recognizes Jesus, the Son of Mary, as a historical figure and history as central to Christianity; however, Christ is more than history and reality is not identical with history.[71] Panikkar argues that to equate Christ with Jesus would be to "reduce Christianity to a mere historical phenomenon."[72]

The acute problem that immediately emerges as a result of Panikkar's interpretation of the Christ Event is the threatened universality and uniqueness of Jesus. Panikkar's position hardly seems compatible with traditional Christian thought: "Indeed, even though there may be so-called gods in heaven or on earth - as in fact there are many gods and many lords - yet for us there is one God, the Father, from whom all things and for whom we exist, and one Lord, Jesus Christ, through whom are all things and through whom we exist."[73] Commenting on this text, John Paul II states that the "one God and one Lord are asserted by way of contrast to the multitude of 'gods' and 'lords' commonly accepted."[74]

D. Is a New Ecumenical
Religion Being Advocated?

In his earlier writings Panikkar did not intend to move away from Roman Catholicism towards a new ecumenical religion. His initial intent was first, to speak the truth about the religious experience of the non-Christian religions, especially the Hindu Advaita Vedanta system and Buddhism, two religions very close to his heart and indeed his own spiritual growth. Secondly, immersed in what he termed a Catholic "orthodox" upbringing in his early years, he gradually became aware of the need to broaden the horizon of his Catholic faith. He felt locked into a narrow church and religion that historically has been unjust to the great religious systems of the world. It saddened him that Christians have been very offensive and "unchristian" in their attitude to the world religions.

His passionate desire to see Christians probe the symbols and rich mythical language of the East has situated him within the heart of Eastern religious traditions in a manner that has at times appeared problematic to fellow Christians. Of course, he has not been alone in his cry for a deeper appreciation of all religious myths,[75] including those of Christianity.

With the passion of a life dedicated to the Catholic priesthood and with the force of hereditary attachment to Hinduism, Panikkar has explored new possibilities within his own Catholic Christian tradition in which to voice interfaith truths never before uttered with such force.

In the process of clearly stating that Hinduism and Buddhism have something important to say about how God has been and is being experienced, Panikkar has charted new ways of conceptualizing Christianity. One such way is intrareligious dialogue.[76] Another is emphasising the need for a theology of religion. Panikkar then draws on the essence of the Christian tradition by proposing the Trinity as the context for acknowledging authentic experiences of God in other religious systems.

He then goes on to propose that it is not enough to speak of the Trinity in solely Christian categories, although he has vastly amplified these categories. In speaking of Isvara as Christ, Panikkar shifts into an arena that gradually breaks with traditional Christian categories of the Trinity. Granted that even this earlier notion of the Trinity is already radical, he still formulates what can be perceived as an extrapolation of the Christian concept of the Trinity. The break is very subtle and hardly noticeable in the first edition of his *The Unknown Christ of Hinduism* (1964); the idea of the fullness of Christ in Jesus reflected in this earlier text tends to camouflage the departure from Christian tradition that Panikkar is developing in relation to the Blessed Trinity. His later edition of that same work (1981) betrays the break with traditional Christian categories more clearly. Jesus no longer emerges as the fullness of Christ. Although Jesus is one of the many Christs in his earlier text, Panikkar makes a further shift in the second edition of his text. He eliminates any notion of Jesus being the fullness of Christ, present in Christianity and hidden in Hinduism. In a very subtle way a further reduction of Jesus of Nazareth emerges.

Prior to 1981 it is evident that Panikkar is not advocating a new ecumenical religion. What he is saying, however, is certainly new and reflects an "ecumenical ecumenism"[78] that is novel.

His 1978 work, *The Intrareligious Dialogue*, along with numerous articles, including several chapters in *Myth, Faith, and Hermeneutics*, recounts the struggle with and critique of traditional Christianity that he was addressing in the seventies. Panikkar is not alone in this critique.

In searching for a global theology, Wilfred Cantwell Smith found "theological activity in the West both dangerously inbred and arrogant in its ignorance of world religious life."[79]

While Panikkar's advocates praise his trinitarian thought,[80] his Christology emerges as suspect. It is acknowledged that he has ploughed through fertile territory in his consideration of the world religions with respect to the Trinity. However, in the process he has tampered with the foundations of Christianity with damaging repercussions.[81]

Subsequently, Panikkar embarks on a further exploration of philosophical categories. With his scientifically analytical mind, he examines the social, cultural and religious categories of history throughout the ages. The section "Cosmotheandric Intuition"[82] in his brilliant article *Colligite Fragmenta:* For an Integration of Reality" marks a new development from his earlier treatment of cosmotheandrism.[83]

This article's attempt to formulate humankind's universal religious experience in a concise form projects the beginnings of a new ecumenical religion, taking into account not only the great systems of the world religions but all experiences of humanity from the earliest primitive states to that of the more sophisticated forms of understanding and worship. The subtle shifting of Panikkar's theology begins to germinate with some clarity in the mid-seventies towards a new ecumenical religion, without, however, completely abandoning Christian doctrines. Even the atheistic world finds a place in his new ecumenical religion.

Panikkar's works achieve a new plateau in the eighties. Although his global outreach goes far beyond traditional Christianity and embraces what appears to be a new ecumenical religion, his outreach never veers from a trinitarian context. This is clearly seen in his 1989 *Gifford Lectures'* crystallization of his earlier thought.

In exploring whether Panikkar is advocating a new ecumenical religion, it is useful also to examine his understanding of the problem of suffering. He sees the social and economic situation of the world today as "desperate" and many of the religious myths as inadequate:

> There really is no issue of "development" for the famine-plagued masses - over half the world's population . . . Today the heavenly paradise, or the collective Utopia, or the glittering "good life", have all lost their grip on the people. A life of privation here, a vale of tears now, a bad karma in this life so that I may be rewarded later on with a heavenly Garden, a city of Brahman, a vision of God or a more comfortable rebirth - all these are rapidly receding myths.[84]

Panikkar is weary of the God and Gods who appear to do little for today's suffering and alienated. He reacts by presenting religion in a manner that it is more accessible and meaningful to the contemporary world and also more at one with humankind, the cosmos and the Divine. It is out of this context that his new ecumenical religion is to be understood.

Panikkar states that the contemporary person needs to "rediscover with a higher degree of awareness . . . that the three dimensions, the Divine, the Cosmic and the Human, belong to the real and they interpenetrate each other, so that everything has anthropomorphic features, as well as divine and material dimensions."[85] He is willing to reinterpret Christianity, Hinduism or any of the world religions in light of this new awareness and interrelationship between the Divine, the cosmic and the human. However, it would appear that the result is not just a renewed Christianity, but rather a new ecumenical holistic movement attempting to incorporate elements from the whole of reality. This effort, of course, requires according to Panikkar new myths which have yet to emerge. Its obvious flaw appears to be a lack of foundation, a lack of rootedness, a lack of history.

His statement that "only the mystic will survive"[86] represents a striving towards something good, something deep and something that includes elements from all experiences, both religious and secular. Panikkar's trinitarian theology in light of his dialogue with the world religions points to the emergence of what appears to be a new ecumenical religion free from Western and Christian dominance.

E. Is the Traditional Understanding of Missiology Undermined?[87]

From his earliest to his latest works Panikkar he has been in constant dialogue with the world of missiology. His passionate critique of the way Christian missionaries have dealt with the religious experiences and expressions of adherents of the various world religions has deeply influenced the development of his trinitarian thought.

Panikkar's appeal to Christianity to remove itself from its cocoon and enter the real world of religious experience with all its diversity has had a deep bearing on his evaluation of Christianity's relationship to the great religious systems of the world. His plea came from the depths of the soul of one whose father breathed into his life the Hindu experience of God with its own set of terms, images and experiences.

The effect was a transformation of the person. Panikkar was not a Christian standing in foreign territory, puzzled by the "truths" of other religions in their own unique cultures and confronted head-on by what appeared to be contrary to traditional Christian teachings. Rather, he realized that he could be Hindu and Christian at the same time. In addition, he discovered pathways into the heart of Buddhism. The young Panikkar became the missionary *par excellence*. Missiology took on a new shape within his soul. He began his main critique of missionary action with an attack on categories which he termed "utilization"[88] and "interpretation."[89] He pointed to the need for a "category of growth,"[90] as the only possible direction for Christians to take in their relationship with the other religious systems. Panikkar's was only one voice among many calling for a different attitude towards the world religions. However, his experience was unique. He was speaking a language from the heart, more than from the head.

While Panikkar was adopting this new positive attitude toward Hinduism, he felt that his new religious awareness was being contradicted by many Christian theologians and missionaries. The Hindu Gods he so loved were being ridiculed, even to the point of being called objects of idolatrous worship. The Hindu Gods of death and destruction were not understood for the value they represent and the importance they hold in the lives of those who worship them.

Panikkar hit upon a dimension which crystallized his trinitarian thought. From his earlier trinitarian framework a new bearing on missiology had emerged. In none of his writings is conversion to Christianity encouraged. One of his earliest texts on the Trinity, *The Trinity and the Religious Experience of Man* (1973), stated that what Christians refer to as the Trinity can be deeply felt in such non-Christian settings as Advaita Vedanta, or Nirvana or within still other categories of religious experiences, for example, the Bhakti school of loving devotion.

During this period Panikkar was calling for deeper participation in one's individual religion and in what he termed intrareligious dialogue, which means sharing another person's religion in its depth. This dialogue was not meant to be simply crossing over from one religion to another, while experiencing only bits of each. Panikkar was urging Christians as well as Hindus and Buddhists to enter into the core of the other religion or religious system with a kind of totality.

In Panikkar's later thinking, which reacts against all theism, especially monotheism, the question of missiology in the traditional Christian sense has become totally irrelevant.[91] This does not mean that every kind of missiology is to be rejected. Missiology needs to be viewed from new perspectives, with the authentic nature of each cultural religious experience being nurtured and valued within its own historical, cultural and religious expression.

What Panikkar stated very bluntly was that Christians had no right converting those of other religions to Christianity, as if Christianity had the fullness of the expression of the Godhead, while other religions had only a reflection or "rays of light" of that truth so clearly expressed in Christianity.

The Pope, discussing the difficulties associated with missiology, made this appeal: "I earnestly ask theologians and professional Christian journalists to intensify the service they render to the Church's mission in order to discover the deep meaning of their work, along the sure path of 'thinking with the Church' (*sentire cum Ecclesia*)."[92]

Panikkar's trinitarian theology would definitely not qualify as "thinking with the Church." His thought represents a new and different movement in Christology and trinitarian theology. If accepted by the Church, it would change the direction of traditional missiology substantially. There are important repercussions of Panikkar's trinitarian thought on traditional Catholic missiology: a) conversion, b) culture and inculturation, c) the question of dialogue with those of other religions, and d) the Second Vatican Council's mandate to increase missionary activity.

First, Panikkar's trinitarian thought has a clear bearing on the question of conversion. He is definitely against the narrow, fundamentalistic form of missionary activity that has characterized much of traditional missiology. This is explained in his critique of "interpretation" and "utilization." Panikkar is not against continuous conversion that leads to growth in the human person. However, stimulus towards growth exist not only in Christianity but can be found in other religious traditions or even in the secular world. His belief that one can come to an experience of the Trinity through any one of the many Christs or more accurately through the homeomorphic equivalents of what Christians refer to as Christ is foundational to his thought. Panikkar champions continuing conversion but not what he perceives as Christian proselytism.

Secondly, the question of culture and inculturation also has significant bearing on missiology. In Panikkar's earliest treatment of the Trinity it is obvious that he was gripped by the relevance of culture and inculturation in religious growth. In fact, it was the new consciousness of his own cultural roots and his desire for the Roman Catholic Church to be more aware of the importance of inculturation that somewhat shaped the development of his own trinitarian thought.

Mission today involves the incarnating of the Gospel in countries of diverse cultures and religions. The need for inculturation has always been important; however, in the present religious consciousness it is an urgent problem. Recently the Holy Father has described inculturation as "the intimate transformation of authentic cultural values through their integration in Christianity and the insertion of Christianity in the various human cultures."[93]

Panikkar would caution that the process of inculturation is multidirectional and is not limited to the insertion of Christianity into other cultures but includes the insertion and sharing of the rich, universal life of the various other religions into Christianity. This would allow for clearer understanding and deeper experiencing of the homeomorphic equivalents of religious symbols and concepts present in the world religions. Panikkar would be in hearty agreement with the Church's new awareness and appreciation of the riches of other cultures and with the growing movement towards inculturation. His trinitarian understanding would foster not only inculturation in the sense of Christianity being inserted into other cultures and religions such as Hinduism but also vice versa. Panikkar would recognize the importance of the Hindu, Buddhist or Moslem having a responsibility towards inculturation in order to enjoy access to the spiritual wealth present in Christian religious systems as well as in Western culture in general.

In his Encyclical on mission the Pope goes on to state, "Inculturation must involve the whole people of God, and not just a few experts, since the people reflect the authentic 'sensus fidei' which must never be lost sight of."[94] Because of Panikkar's holistic approach in the formation of his trinitarian theology, he would interpret the "whole people of God" to include all who experience the Godhead, regardless of religion and the unique position in which they are immersed. This is broader than the Roman Catholic meaning of "the people of God" who, strictly speaking, are only baptized Christians.[95] Those of other religions are only potentially "the visible people of God."

The Church sees inculturation as planting the seeds of Christianity within other cultures and religious systems in order that its expression will be more integrated and its content understood in a more harmonious way than that presented by missionaries in the past. Panikkar's trinitarian thought, which in a sense represents the core of his theology of religions, requires that inculturation must be checked if it means dominance or imperialism on the part of Christianity. He has high praise for exchange and interrelationship between cultures. However, he would definitely oppose using cultural categories to inject Christianity within other religious systems with the supposition that Christianity enjoys the fullness of the revelation of the Godhead, while other religions such as Hinduism and Buddhism bear only some reflection of the Godhead to the extent that adherents of these other religions possess Christian values or are "anonymous Christians" in their worship and lived experience.

Quite often a statement can be interpreted in different ways. An example would be the following assertion of the Holy Father: [Inculturation] "will require an incubation of the Christian 'mystery' in the genius of your people in order that its native voice, more clearly and frankly, may then be raised harmoniously in the chorus of the other voices in the universal church."[96]

Because Panikkar understands Church in a universal sense, as extending beyond the parameters of Christianity, with the Trinity at the centre, he could accept "the chorus of the other voices" as including other religious systems which have a voice equal[97] to Christianity. However, according to the Holy Father "the chorus of the other voices in the universal church" applies directly to Christianity. Christianity would give a brighter glow to what was already present as a reflection of the light of Christianity.

The third of the many difficult problems in the area of missionary activity is the question of dialogue. Here as well, Panikkar's concept of Trinity has a bearing.

Today dialogue is one of the main avenues of missionary activity. Panikkar has stated that dialogue has become the most rewarding exchange of spiritual awareness in a universal setting. His earlier as well as his later thought on the Trinity has developed out of dialogue between the world religions, not only on the level of sharing concepts, various experiences and expressions of faith, but also on the level of intrareligious dialogue taking place deep in the hearts of individuals encountering the universal Trinity. There emerges from the world religions a hybrid experience and expression of the Trinity within the individual where dialogue ceases to be dialogue as intimate communion with the Divine takes place.

Missionary activity in the Church today still functions primarily on the level of interreligious dialogue. In the words of the Holy Father:

> Inter-religious dialogue is a part of the Church's evangelizing mission . . . This mission, in fact, is addressed to those who do not know Christ and his Gospel, and who belong for the most part to other religions . . . [Christ] does not fail to make himself present in many ways, not only to individuals but also to entire peoples through their spiritual riches, of which their religions are the main and essential expression, even when they contain "gaps, insufficiencies and errors."[98]

Since the Second Vatican Council the Church has clearly acknowledged awareness of the presence of Christ in other religions, as the above statement indicates. However, the "gaps, insufficiencies and errors" would be interpreted differently by Panikkar. He is very critical of the limitations within all religions, including Christianity. He does not see dialogue as addressed to those "who do not know Christ." Rather, Panikkar sees dialogue as addressed to those who have experienced and given expression to the Trinity within the milieu of their own culture and religion. Furthermore, he maintains that at times this experience of non-Christians may be far more profound than that of Christians and that they may sometimes be in a more grace-filled position to reflect the Trinity than Christians who might hold that because of the Good News of Jesus Christ they are automatically in a better and more authoritative position to discover "gaps" and "insufficiencies" and condemn "errors" in non-Christian religions.

The fourth problem to be considered in this section is the Church's mandate to increase missionary activity. This mandate has become even more urgent for John Paul II, who writes: "My direct contact with peoples who do not know Christ has convinced me even more of the *urgency of missionary activity*."[99] The Holy Father points out the importance of The Second Vatican Council's emphasis on the Church's missionary nature, which is based "in a dynamic way on the Trinitarian mission itself."[100]

The Church's official teaching is reflected in the Pope's first Encyclical: "the Church's fundamental function in every age, and particularly in ours, is to direct man's gaze, to point the awareness and experience of the whole of humanity towards the mystery of Christ."[101] The universal mission of the Church is "born of faith in Jesus Christ, as is stated in our Trinitarian profession of faith: 'I believe in one Lord, Jesus Christ, the only Son of God, eternally begotten of the Father . . . For us men and for our salvation he came down from heaven: by the power of the Holy Spirit he became incarnate from the Virgin Mary, and was made man.' "[102]

In addressing current issues in missiology, the Holy Father raises some questions similar to those with which Panikkar has struggled: "*Is missionary work among non-Christians still relevant?* Has it not been replaced by inter-religious dialogue? . . . Is it not possible to attain salvation in any religion?"[103]

Panikkar, however, raises the questions from a completely different perspective from that of the Pope. While John Paul II sees the need to reinforce traditional teachings of Christianity, Panikkar sees just the opposite. In spite of what appears to be a crisis in missiology, as reflected in some of its current questions, John Paul II urges missionaries to forge ahead with the mandate to preach Jesus Christ to adherents of non-Christian religions as well as to others in the secular non-religious world.

What followers of traditional Christianity would hold as major problems, Panikkar would recognize in many instances as enlightened horizons which can bring new awareness to adherents of non-Christian religious systems, and more importantly to Christians themselves. In Panikkar's wide range of religious and secular thought, it is his novel concept of Christ and his own understanding of the trinitarian reality that enable Christians to rediscover new depths as they engage in missionary activity.

For Panikkar missionary action is not a one-way movement of religious truths directed to those who live mainly in darkness, but rather a mutual sharing of truths that constitutes what he terms intrareligious dialogue and assimilation of growth. He would consider missionary activity still relevant and even necessary but in a very different context from that of the present official Church's position. Panikkar's theology clashes directly with some of the premises of traditional missionary activity.

Notes

1   Bernard Lonergan, *Method in Theology* (New York: Herder and Herder, 1972), 218-219.
2   Gordon Kaufman, *Systematic Theology: A Historicist Perspective* (New York: Charles Scribner's Sons, 1968), 185-186.
3   Edward H. Carr, *What is History?* (New York: Random House, 1961), 24.
4   See Panikkar, "Is History the Measure of Man?", 39-45.
5   *Ibid.*, 39.
6   *Ibid.*
7   See *ibid.*, 35-39.
8   Donald C. Masters, *The Christian Idea of History* (Waterloo: Waterloo Lutheran University, 1962), 33.
9   Masters, *The Christian Idea of History*, 33.
10 *Rig Veda*, 10.121. For commentary see Wendy Doniger O'Flaherty, ed. and trans. *The Rig Veda: An Anthology* (Middlesex: Penguin Books, 1981), 26-29.
11 Prabhavananda, *The Spiritual Heritage of India*, 273.
12 *Ibid.*
13 Arnaldo Momigliano, *The Classical Foundations of Modern Historiography* (Berkeley: University of California Press, 1990), 156. For more information on the origins of ecclesiastical historiography see *ibid.*, 132-152.
14 See Dermot Lane, *The Reality of Jesus* (New York: Paulist Press, 1975), 27.
15 Masters, *The Christian Idea of History*, 34.
16 See Panikkar, "Instead of a Foreword: An Open Letter," vi.
17 Panikkar, "In Christ There Is Neither Hindu nor Christian," 478.
18 *Ibid.*
19 See Panikkar, "Instead of a Foreword: An Open Letter," ix. See also Raimundo Panikkar, "Rtatattva: A Preface to a Hindu-Christian Theology," *Jeevadhara* 9 (1979): 49.
20 See Raimundo Panikkar, "The Texture of a Text: In response to P. Ricoeur," *Point of Contact* 2 (1978): 64. See also Panikkar, "A Preface to a Hindu-Christian Theology," 50-57.
21 Masters, *The Christian Idea of History*, 34.
22 See *ibid.*
23 See Panikkar. "Instead of a Foreword: An Open Letter," xi, xii.
24 John Paul II, *The Mission of Christ the Redeemer*, 119.
25 See Wendy Doniger O'Flaherty, *The Origins of Evil in Hindu Mythology* (Berkeley: University of California Press, 1976) for some of the sources of evil in Hinduism.
26 See *ibid.*
27 See Panikkar, "Instead of a Foreword: An Open Letter," viii.
28 Masters, *The Christian Idea of History*, 34.
29 *Ibid.*

30 Panikkar has a nuanced description of "eschaton." He sees eschatology in terms of "ultimate things" rather than "end times."

31 See Panikkar, "Is History the Measure of Man?" 42.

32 Panikkar has difficulty with all forms of theism.

33 Masters, *The Christian Idea of History*, 34.

34 The Good News is found through the *homeomorphic equivalents* of the various world religions. See Panikkar, "Instead of a Foreword: An Open Letter," xii. The Good News for Panikkar is found even outside the sacred texts.

35 Masters, *The Christian Idea of History*, 34.

36 *Ibid.*

39 Panikkar, *Unknown Christ of Hinduism* (1964), 51. See also *ibid.*, 21 and ix.

40 See *ibid.*, 148-162.

42 See Panikkar, "*Colligite Fragmenta*: For an Integration of Reality," 19.

43 See Panikkar, "Have 'Religions' the Monopoly on *Religion?*", 515-517; for a breakdown of organized religions, 515-516; a redefining of salvation in the context of "making one whole, healthy, free, and complete," 515; and a call for ecumenical ecumenism to act as "a corrective criticism" among the world religions, 217. In 1975 Panikkar uses the phrase "The Threefold Mystery of Reality" to speak of the Trinity with a clear emphasis on the Asian's contribution to awareness of "God" in a "deeper and a more transformed" sense. See Panikkar, "The Universal Contribution of Christian Monasticism in Asia to the Universal Church," 81.

44 Panikkar, "For an Integration of Reality," 19.

46 See Panikkar, "In Christ There is Neither Hindu or Christisn," 475.

47 The word "seemingly" is used to note that in reality he does not by-pass the Christ Event. What he does is by-pass Jesus as the one and only Christ.

48 See the following: Panikkar, *Unknown Christ of Hinduism* (1964); Panikkar, "Confrontation between Hinduism and Christ" (1968): 197-204; Panikkar, "Instead of a Foreword: An Open Letter," v-xiv; Panikkar, "Reader's Response," 80.

49 See Panikkar, "Confrontation between Hinduism and Christ" (1969), 197.

50 The Vatican II document, *Nostra Aetate*, on non-Christian religions was one serious attempt to deal with the religious experiences of other religions.

51 See Panikkar, *Unknown Christ of Hinduism* (1964), 119-131.

52 Panikkar, "Confrontation between Hinduism and Christ" (1969), 202.

53 *Ibid.*

54 John Paul II, *The Mission of Christ the Redeemer*, 13. This encyclical has been chosen as the reference point in this section because it is the most recent utterance on the topic at such a high level of the ordinary papal magisterium.

55 Acts 4: 10, 12.

56 See John Paul II, *The Mission of Christ the Redeemer*, 13.

57 Mt. 16:16.

58 See Panikkar, "Confrontation between Hinduism and Christ" (1969), 202.

59 See Panikkar, *Unknown Christ of Hinduism* (1964), 121. See also Panikkar, "Confrontation between Hinduism and Christ," 202.

60 Panikkar, "Confrontation between Hinduism and Christ," 203.

61 *Ibid.*, 204.

62 John Paul II, *The Mission of Christ the Redeemer*, 15. The emphasis on *only* is that of the Pope.

63 David Tracy, *Dialogue with the Other: The Inter-Religious Dialogue* (Louvain: Peeters Press, 1991), 85.

64 Panikkar, "In Christ There is Neither Hindu nor Christian," 479.

65 Some indications of this are evident in Raimundo Panikkar, "Christianity and World Religions," in *Christianity*, Collective Work (Patiala, India: Punjabi University, 1969), 78-127. This apparent break is seen in Raimundo Panikkar, "The Category of Growth in Comparative Religion: A Critical Self-Examination," *Harvard Theological Review* 66 (1973): 113-140; also in Panikkar, *Salvation in Christ: Concreteness and Universality, the Supername.* Most of the content of the preceeding work was published as Panikkar, "The Meaning of Christ's Name in the Universal Economy of Salvation." See also Panikkar, *Unknown Christ of Hinduism* (1981).

66 See Panikkar, "Reader's Response," 80. See also Panikkar, "Instead of a Foreword: An Open Letter," v-xiv.

67 Panikkar, "Reader's Response," (1989), 80.

68 Several authors have claimed that Panikkar has not dealt adequately with the historical Jesus. For example, see: Robert Smet, *Essai sur la pensée de Raimundo Panikkar: Une contribution indienne à la théologie des religions et à la christologie* (Louvain-la-Neuve: Centre d'histoire des religions, 1981), 105; Geffré, "La foi à l'âge du pluralisme religieux," 810. Dupuis, *Jesus Christ at the Encounter of World Religions*, 184-189.

69 Panikkar, "Instead of a Foreword: An Open Letter" (1988), xii.

70 See Panikkar, "Confrontation between Hinduism and Christ," 204.

71 See Panikkar. "Instead of a Foreword: An Open Letter," xii.

72 *Ibid.*, xiii.

73 I Cor 8: 5-6.

74 John Paul II, *The Mission of Christ the Redeemer*, 13.

75 One author argues that "we have lost . . . our own myths . . . This loss becomes the more apparent when we see how other cultures preserve their myths in ways inaccessible to us, given our cultural definitions of fluidity and felicity." Wendy Doniger O'Flaherty, *Other Peoples' Myths: The Cave of Echoes* (New York: Macmillan Publishing Co., 1988), 5.

76 See Panikkar, *Intrareligious Dialogue*, 28, 34, 40, 52, and *passim*.

78 See Panikkar, *Intrareligious Dialogue*, 3, 4.

79 Edward I. Hughes, *Wilfred Cantwell Smith: A Theology for the World* (London: SCM Press, 1986), 164.

80   Among the authors praising Panikkar's contribution are the following. M.M. Thomas states in the Foreword to one of Panikkar's trinitarian works, "He is recognized as an original thinker who has advanced the theology of inter-religious relation along new and fruitfully creative lines." Panikkar, *The Trinity and World Religions* (1970), v. Harold Coward views Panikkar's concept of Trinity as "a junction where the authentic spiritual dimension of all religions meet within christian thought." Coward, *Pluralism: Challenge to World Religions*, 53. Cousins comments, "Not only does Panikkar's trinitarian approach provide a model for pluralistic dialogue but it situates the dialogue primarily in the realm of spirituality and not in that of dogmatic formulation or metaphysical speculation." Cousins, "Trinity and World Religions," 482. Referring to Panikkar's *Trinity and Religious Experience*, Rowan Williams affirms that it is "one of the best and least read meditations on the Trinity in our century." Williams, "Trinity and Pluralism," 3. Also see Devdas, "The Theandrism of Raimundo Panikkar and Trinitarian Parallels in Modern Hindu Thought," 617.

81   Theologians have negatively critiqued Panikkar in varying degrees. Ewert Cousins, who has often praised Panikkar's contribution to trinitarian thought, states that in the "Logos dimension of his trinitarian theology and in his extended essay on the Supername," Panikkar's "Christology has not reached the mature crystallization of his trinitarian theology." He continues, "Although this early work has been fruitful, for some years now I have felt that Panikkar was not moving in the right direction. From my point of view the crucial problem of an ecumenical Christology is precisely its particularity." Cousins, "Raimundo Panikkar and the Christian Systematic Theology of the Future," 148-149. Jacques Dupuis states, " . . . Panikkar makes a dangerous distinction between the Mystery and the Jesus myth - that is, the Christ of faith and the Jesus of history. He surely seems to separate them as objects of faith and belief, respectively. Is a reduction of the Jesus myth to an object of belief as distinct from faith compatible with the Christian profession of faith in the person from Nazareth? And as if by backlash, is not the content of faith reduced to a vague, neutral relationship to a transcendence, empty in its own turn, and as without an object? Is it not itself reduced to a myth, an abstraction?" Dupuis, *Jesus Christ at the Encounter of World Religions*, 187.

82   See Panikkar, *"Colligite Fragmenta*: For an Integration of Reality," 68-91.

83   See Panikkar, *Trinity and Religious Experience*, 69-80.

84   Panikkar, "Is History the Measure of Man?" 42.

85   Raimon Panikkar, "Anima mundi- vita hominis - spiritus dei. Some aspects of Cosmotheandric Spirituality," in *Actualitas omnium actuum,* ed. Erwin Schadel (Frankfurt: Verlag Peter Lang, 1989), 354.

86   *Ibid.*

87   This section will constitute, for the most part, not explicit statements from Panikkar, but conclusions drawn by the author from Panikkar's premises. For a concise statement on Panikkar's treatment of the future of mission see Raimundo Panikkar, "Regard sur l'avenir de la mission" in *Église et Mission* 234 (1984): 2-11.

88   See Panikkar, *Intrareligious Dialogue*, 58.

89   *Ibid.*, 62.

90   *Ibid.*, 69.

91   See Panikkar, "Theism/ Monotheism," in *Gifford Lectures*, No. 3.

92   John Paul II, *The Mission of Christ the Redeemer*, 52-53.

93   John Paul II, paraphrase by International Theological Commission, Extraordinary Assembly of 1985, *Final Report*, ii, D, 4 (Cited in John Paul II, *The Mission of Christ The Redeemer*, 77). For entire document see *International Theological Commission. Texts and Documents. 1969-1985*, ed. Michael Sharkey (San Francisco: Ignatius Press, 1989), 280.

94   John Paul II, *The Mission of Christ the Redeemer*, 80.

95   See Vatican II, Dogmatic Constitution on the Church, *Lumen Gentium*, par. 13-16.

96   Paul VI, *Address* to those participating in the Symposium of African Bishops at Kampala, July 31, 1969, *Acta Apostolicae Sedis* 61 (1969): 577.

97   "Equal" used not necessarily in the strict sense of equality, rather in the sense of the authentic value of each to be recognized without Christianity as dominant.

98   John Paul II, *The Mission of Christ the Redeemer*, 81.

99   *Ibid.*

100 *Ibid.*, 8.

101 *Ibid.*, 12.

102 *Ibid.*

103 *Ibid.*, 12-13.

Conclusion

The theology of the Trinity proposed by Raimon Panikkar in his earlier thought was an attempt to bring the revelation of the Blessed Trinity to the world in a manner that recognizes the authenticity of the religious experience of adherents of both Hinduism and Buddhism. Panikkar's later and radical theory of the Trinity, however, appears less compatible with the traditional Christian concept of the Trinity. In his later thought he appears to break substantially with the foundational anchor of Christianity, which is Jesus Christ. Although this is more evident in Panikkar's later writings, traces of it can be found even as far back as the early edition of his *The Unknown Christ of Hinduism* (1964). His theology of the radical Trinity, though containing much truth about universal human experience, appears to lack the basic tenets of the Christian faith in which the Trinity is revealed principally through the life, death and resurrection of Jesus Christ. To propose a treatise on the Trinity without Jesus Christ the Risen Lord as central, appears to be something other than an elucidation of the Trinity professed by Christians.

Although Panikkar's theory of the universal Trinity suffers from serious limitations, there are several important positive elements that he has highlighted in his attempt to formulate a new trinitarian concept that is truly universal and that resonates with religious experiences outside the parameters of Christianity. Basically there are three areas where Professor Panikkar has forged ahead to provide insights and associations, either completely original or at least unprecedented in their impact.

First, although the later Panikkar will radically transform his thought on the Trinity, in his early period he already disclosed a refreshing breakthrough from a limited trinitarian vision, which had little bearing on the world religions. He accomplished this by seeing a) Nirvana, as the reflection of the apophatic dimension of the Father and b) the non-duality of the Advaita Vedanta as the reflection of the experience of the Holy Spirit.

The theology of the Trinity proposed by Panikkar underlines the validity of religious encounters within these great world religions. Although Vatican II speaks only of "rays of light" in connection with the world religions, Panikkar's trinitarian framework insists that the pulse of God's presence in the world beats steadily within the heart of each of the great world religions.

He also asserts clearly that Christianity should not lay claim to an exclusive experience of the Trinity. Christians emphasize only one dimension of the experience of the trinitarian mystery, and one should look to the other great religious systems of the world to discover other ways of encountering the triune God. Through his trinitarian concept Panikkar exalts the experiential systems of the world religions, especially Hinduism and Buddhism. Unfortunately, his treatment has not proven adequately satisfying to the Western Christian.

The second area of significant contribution to the world of inter-faith dialogue is Panikkar's notion of the Trinity as seen within the Advaita Vedanta system, where Isvara is the Christ, leading Advaitins to a deeper realization of the trinitarian Godhead. Although this particular aspect of Panikkar's thought has met with major criticism in Christian theological centres, especially because of the place of Jesus of Nazareth in Panikkar's trinitarian framework, nevertheless his theology contains valuable elements.

His generous treatment of the Gods of the Eastern religions raises them to the level of Jesus. Although this has caused utter dismay for many Christian theologians, Panikkar's statement is significant. The Gods of the world religions are extremely important in the discovery of how other cultures and religions respond to the trinitarian mystery. Panikkar also attempts to show that the Gods are to be understood, not in the context of what they are in themselves, but rather in the way they are experienced and according to the role they assume in the increased understanding and consciousness of adherents of non-Christian religions, as they come to a deeper awareness of the trinitarian mystery.

The third area of significant contribution in Panikkar's trinitarian system is his concept of non-duality as it relates to the secular sphere. The concept traces the history of human experience transcending the secular world in order for a deeper dimension of the experience of the Trinity to emerge.

Panikkar is immensely proud of his latest trinitarian theology, which encompasses all religions, all of humanity and even the entire cosmos. He now considers his earlier trinitarian thought to be lacking in maturity and depth. Yet, his earlier treatment already pinpointed the complexity and intricacy of the various world religions, together with the problems Christians encounter, as they seek to understand God's communication to adherents of non-Christian religions and cultures, vastly different from the Western world.

Nevertheless, Panikkar's mature trinitarian position tends to generalize and universalize to the extent that the religious dimension appears to fade dramatically into a vague universal trinitarian mystery, which ceases to find anchorage within any religious tradition, much less Christianity, or, more precisely, in the life, death and resurrection of Jesus Christ.

Panikkar has used the trinitarian concept as a heuristic tool in searching out new ways to give validity to the religious experience of the world religions and at the same time to widen and deepen the Christian notion of the Trinity. In some ways he has succeeded; however, since his trinitarian system can exist without rootedness in Jesus Christ, it appears overall that he has taken a turn in his journey that only with great difficulty can be called Christian.

Professor Panikkar has spoken a most courageous word in defense of the various world religions and of the depth experience of all humans, even those belonging to no formal religion. The road along which he has led his readers and others with whom he has come into contact can only point to a "breakthrough" in the discovery of how Christians can lessen their stammering as they continue speaking about the divine mystery of the Blessed Trinity.

In the pursuit of a more relevant vision of the Trinity in light of modern religious and historical consciousness, Panikkar has spurred three important areas of dialogue: a) intrareligious dialogue, i.e., within the hearts of believers; b) interreligious dialogue, which has generated new insights among the living world religions; and c) lastly, dialogue among Christian theologians and Church leaders struggling with questions never faced heretofore at such depth.

The major flaw throughout the development of Panikkar's trinitarian thought lies in his treatment of the place of Jesus Christ in relation to the

Trinity. Although Raimon Panikkar has been considerably successful in his attempt to universalize the concept of Trinity, he has done so at the cost of undermining certain foundational aspects of the Christian theology of the Blessed Trinity.

Select Bibliography

I. Primary Sources

Books by Raimon Panikkar
(in chronological order)

The Unknown Christ of Hinduism. London: Darton, Longman and Todd, 1964.

Kerygma und Indien. Zur heilsgeschichtlichen Problematik der christlichen Begegnung mit Indien. Hamburg: Herbert Reich, 1967.

Le mystère du culte dans l'Hindouisme et le Christianisme. Paris: Édition du Cerf, 1970.

The Trinity and World Religions. Icon- Person-Mystery. Madras: Christian Literature Society, 1970.

Salvation in Christ: Concreteness and Universality, the Supername. Santa Barbara: privately published, 1972.

Worship and Secular Man. An essay on the liturgical nature of Man, considering Secularization as a major phenomenon of our time and Worship as an apparent fact of all times. A study towards an integral anthropology. Maryknoll: Orbis Books, 1973.

The Trinity and the Religious Experience of Man. Icon-Person-Mystery. London: Darton, Longman and Todd, 1973. This is a revised edition of *The Trinity and World Religions* (1970).

The Vedic Experience. Mantramanjari: An Anthology of the Vedas for Modern Man and Contemporary Celebration. Berkeley: University of California Press, 1977.

The Intrareligious Dialogue. New York: Paulist Press, 1978.

Myth, Faith and Hermeneutics. New York: Paulist Press, 1979.

The Unknown Christ of Hinduism: Towards an Ecumenical Christophany. Maryknoll: Orbis Books, 1981. This is a revised edition of *The Unknown Christ of Hinduism* (1964).

Blessed Simplicity. The Monk as Universal Archetype. New York: Seabury Press, 1982.

The Silence of God. The Answer of the Buddha. Maryknoll: Orbis Books, 1989.

On Catholic Identity. Warren Lecture Series in Catholic Studies No. 17. Tulsa: University of Tulsa, 1991.

The Cosmotheandric Experience. Emerging Religious Consciousness. Maryknoll: Orbis Books, 1993.

Selected Articles (and Chapters in Books)
by Raimon Panikkar
(in chronological order)

"Mission of the Laity in the Church." *The King's Rally* 34 (1957): 123-129.

"Some Phenomenological Aspects of Hindu Spirituality Today." *Oriental Thought* 3 (Oct. 1957): 157-191.

"Common Grounds for Christian - Non -Christian Collaboration." *Religion and Society* 5 (March 1958): 29-36.

"The Existential Phenomenology of Truth." *Philosophy Today* 2 (Spring 1958): 13-21.

"The Integration of Indian Philosophical and Religious Thought." *Religion and Society* 5 (June 1958): 22-29.

"Contemporary Hindu Spirituality." *Philosophy Today* 3 (Summer 1959): 112-127.

"Isvara and Christ as a Philosophical Problem." *Religion and Society* 6 (Oct. 1959): 1-9.

"Letters from Holy Mount Athos." *Sobornost* 4 (1965): 726-731.

"The Crisis of Madhyamika and Indian Philosophy Today." *Philosophy East and West* 16 (July-Oct. 1966): 117-131.

"Dialogue between Ian and Ray: Is Jesus Christ Unique?" *Theoria to Theory* 1 (Jan. 1967): 127-137.

"Toward an Ecumenical Theandric Spirituality." *Journal of Ecumenical Studies* 5 (1968): 507-534.

"The Internal Dialogue: The Insufficiency of the so-called Phenomenological Epoché in Religious Encounter." *Religion and Society* 4 (1968): 55-66.

"Confrontation Between Hinduism and Christ." *New Blackfriars* 50 (Jan. 1969): 197-204.

"Christianity and World Religions." In *Christianity*, Collective Work, 78-127. Patiala, India: Punjabi University, 1969.

"Secularization and Worship - a Bibliography." *Studia Liturgica* 7 (1970): 131-141.

"Indirect Methods in Missionary Apostolates: Some Theological Reflections." *Indian Journal of Theology* 19 (July-Dec. 1970): 111-113.

"Technology and Future in a Theological Perspective." *Anticipation* 12 (1970): 18-20.

"Nirvana and the Awareness of the Absolute." In *The God Experience*, ed. Joseph P. Whelan, 81-99. New York: Newman Press, 1971.

"Are the Old Forms of Prayer Dying?" *The Lamp* 69 (Nov. 1971): 11-31.

"Il messagio dell'India di ieri al mondo di oggi." *Filosofia* 22 (Jan. 1971): 3-28.

"Christ, Abel and Melchizedech: The Church and non-Abrahamic religions." *Jeevadhara* 1 (Sept.-Oct. 1971): 391- 403.

"Faith: a Constitutive Dimension of Man." *Journal of Ecumenical Studies* 8 (Spring 1971): 223-254.

"The Rules of the Game in the Religious Encounter." *The Journal of Religious Studies* 3 (1971): 12-16.

"Some Aspects of Suffering and Sorrow in the Vedas." *Jeevadhara* 2 (Sept.-Oct. 1972): 387-398.

"The God of Silence." *Indian Journal of Theology* 21 (Jan.-June 1972): 116-124.

"The Meaning of Christ's Name in the Universal Economy of Salvation." In *Evangelization, Dialogue and Development*, ed. Mariasusai Dhavamony, 195-218. Rome: Università Gregoriana Editrice, 1972.

"The Ultimate Experience." *Theology Digest* 20 (Autumn 1972): 219-226.

"Christians and the So-called Non-Christians." *Cross Currents* 22 (Summer-Fall, 1972): 281-308.

"The Mirage of the Future." *Teilhard Review* 8 (June 1973): 42-45.

"The Category of Growth in Comparative Religion: A Critical Self-Examination." *Harvard Theological Review* 66 (1973): 113-140.

"The Hindu Ecclesial Consciousness: Some Ecclesiological Reflections." *Jeevadhara* 4 (May-June 1974): 199-205.

"Have 'Religions' the Monopoly on Religion?" *Journal of Ecumenical Studies* 11 (Summer 1974): 515-517.

"The Silence of the Word: Non-dualistic Polarities." *Cross Currents* 24 (Summer-Fall 1974): 154-171.

"Eastern and Western Ways of Thinking about God: An Interview with Raimundo Panikkar." *Listening* 10 (Winter 1975): 18-32.

"The Contribution of Christian Monasticism in Asia to the Universal Church." *Cistercian Studies* 10 (1975): 73-84.

"The Cosmotheandric Vision: An Emerging Consciousness for the Third Millenium A.D." In *Vecchi e Nuovi Dei*, ed. R. Caporale, 521-544. Turin: Valentine, 1976.

"Man as a Ritual Being." *Chicago Studies* 16 (Spring 1977): 5-28.

"*Colligite Fragmenta*: For an Integration of Reality." In *From Alienation to At-one-ness*, ed. F.A. Eigo, 19-91. Philadelphia: Villanova University Press, 1977.

"The New Innocence." *Cross Currents* 27 (Spring 1977): 7-28.

"Time and Sacrifice: The Sacrifice of Time and the Ritual of Modernity." In *The Study of Time III*, ed. J.T. Fraser, 683-727. New York: Springer, 1978.

"Man and His Spirituality." *Forum for Correspondence and Contact* 9 (Jan. 1978): 58-61.

"Non-dualistic Relation between Religion and Politics." *Religion and Society* 25 (Sept. 1978): 53-63.

"The Rhetoric of Intrareligious Dialogue." *Jeevadhara* 8 (Sept. - Oct. 1978): 367-380.

"The Texture of a Text: In Response to Paul Ricoeur." *Point of Contact* 2 (April - May 1978): 51-64.

"The Vitality and Role of Indian Philosophy Today." *Indian Philosophical Quarterly* 5 (July 1978): 673-692.

"The Bostonian Verities: A Comment on the Boston Affirmations." *Andover Newton Quarterly* 18 (Jan. 1978): 145-153.

"Rtatattva: A Preface to a Hindu-Christian Theology." *Jeevadhara* 9 (Jan. - Feb. 1979): 6-63.

"The Myth of Pluralism: The Tower of Babel - A Meditation on Non-Violence." *Cross Currents* 29 (Summer 1979): 197-230.

"Some Words Instead of a Response." *Cross-Currents* 29 (Summer 1979): 193-196.

"Response to Harold Coward." *Cross Currents* 29 (Summer 1979): 190-192.

"Words and Terms." In *Esistenza, Mito, Ermeneutica*, ed. M.M. Olivetti, 117-133. Rome: Istituto di Studi Filosofici, 1980.

"Hermeneutics of Comparative Religion: Paradigms and Models." *Journal of Dharma* 5 (Jan. - March 1980): 38-51.

"Man and Religion: A Dialogue with Panikkar." *Jeevadhara* 11 (Jan. - February 1981): 5-32.

"Is History the Measure of Man?" *The Teilhard Review* 16 (1981): 39-45.

"The Contemplative Mood: A Challenge to Modernity." *Cross Currents* 31 (Fall 1981): 261-272.

"Toward an Ecumenical Ecumenism." *Journal of Ecumenical Studies* 19 (Fall 1982): 781-786.

"Is the Notion of Human Rights a Western Concept?" *Diogene* 120 (Winter 1982): 75-102.

"Letter to Abhishiktananda: On Eastern-Western Monasticism." *Studies in Formative Spirituality* 3 (Nov. 1982): 427-451.

"Catholicity and Ecumenism." *Ecumenical Trends* 12 (Sept. 1983): 113-115.

"The End of History: The Threefold Structure of Human Time-Consciousness." In *Teilhard and the Unity of Knowledge*, ed. Thomas King and James Salmon, 83-141. New York: Paulist Press, 1983.

"Interview." *Epiphany* 3 (Summer 1983): 2-31.

"The Cosmotheandric Intuition." *Jeevadhara* 14 (Jan. 1984): 27-35.

"The Marian Dimensions of Life." *Epiphany* 4 (Summer 1984): 3-9.

"The Destiny of Technological Civilization: The Prophetic Might of an Ancient Buddhist Legend." *Alternatives* 10 (June 1984): 237-253.

"Regard sur l'avenir de la mission." *Église et Mission* 234 (June 1984): 2-11.

"The Dialogical Dialogue." In *The World's Religious Traditions*, ed. Frank Whaling, 61-72. Edinburgh: T. & T. Clark, 1984.

"Religions and Politics: The Western Dilemma." In *Religion and Politics in the Modern World*, ed. Peter H. Merkl and Ninian Smart, 44-60. New York: New York University Press, 1985.

"The Jordan, the Tiber, and the Ganges: Three Kairological Moments of Christic Self-Consciousness." In *The Myth of Christian Uniqueness: Toward a Pluralistic Theology of Religion*, ed. John Hick and Paul Knitter, 89-116. Maryknoll: Orbis Books, 1987.

"Instead of A Foreword: An Open Letter." In *Theological Approach and Understanding of Religions: Jean Daniélou and Raimundo Panikkar. A Study in Contrast.* Dominic Veliath, v-xiv. Bangalore: Kristu Jyoti College, 1988.

"Reader's Response." *International Bulletin of Missionary Research* 13 (April 1989): 80.

"Anima mundi - vita hominis - spiritus dei. Some aspects of Cosmotheandric Spirituality." *In Actualitas omnium actuum*, ed. Erwin Schadel, 341-356. Frankfurt: Peter Lang, 1989.

"In Christ There is Neither Hindu nor Christian: Perspectives on Hindu-Christian Dialogue." In *Religious Issues and Interreligious Dialogues*, ed. C. Wei-hsun Fu and G.E. Spiegler, 475-489. New York: Greenwood Press, 1989.

"A Christophany for Our Times." *Theology Digest* 39 (Spring 1992): 3-21. (35th Annual Robert Cardinal Bellarmine Lecture, St. Louis University, Oct. 9, 1991.)

Unpublished Material by
Raimon Panikkar

Gifford Lectures: Trinity and Atheism: The Housing of the Divine in the Contemporary World. (A series of ten lectures given at University of Edinburgh, under the title of *The Rhythm of Being*, April 25 - May 12, 1989, to be published by Orbis Books.)

II. Secondary Sources

Books, Articles (and Chapters in Books) on
Panikkar or with reference to Panikkar

Baumer - Despeigne, Odette. "A Pilgrimage to One's Own Roots - A Precondition to Religious Dialogue?" In *Interreligious Dialogue: Voices from a New Frontier*, ed. M. Darrol Bryant and Frank Flinn, 65-72. New York: Paragon House, 1989.

Cousins, Ewert. "Introduction: The Panikkar Symposium at Santa Barbara." *Cross Currents* 29 (Summer 1979): 131-134; 140.

_____. "Raimundo Panikkar and the Christian Systematic Theology of the Future." *Cross Currents* 29 (Summer 1979): 141-155.

_____. "The Trinity and World Religions." *Journal of Ecumenical Studies* 7 (Summer 1970): 476-498.

Coward, Harold. "The Dialogical Approach." In *Pluralism: Challenge to World Religions*. Maryknoll: Orbis Books, 1985.

_____. "Panikkar's Approach to Interreligious Dialogue." *Cross Currents* 29 (Summer 1979): 183-189.

D'Costa, Gavin. "Christ, the Trinity and Religious Plurality." In *Christian Uniqueness Reconsidered. The Myth of a Pluralistic Theology of Religions*, ed. Gavin D'Costa, 16-29. Maryknoll: Orbis Books, 1990.

Devdas, Nalini. "The Theandrism of Raimundo Panikkar and Trinitarian Parallels in Modern Hindu Thought." *Journal of Ecumenical Studies* 17 (Fall 1980): 606-620.

Geffré, Claude. "La foi à l'âge du pluralisme religieux." *La vie spirituelle* 143 (Nov.-Dec. 1989): 805-815.

Gorday, Peter. "Raimundo Panikkar: Pluralism Without Relativism." *The Christian Century* 106 (Dec. 1989): 1147-1150.

Kelly, Anthony. *The Trinity of Love: A Theology of the Christian God.* Delaware: Michael Glazier, 1989.

Knitter, Paul. "Raimundo Panikkar: The Universal Christ and the Particular Jesus." In *No Other Name?*, New York: Orbis Books, 1985.

_____. "The Wider Ecumenism: Exploring New Directions." *Ecumenical Trends* 15 (September 1986): 134-137.

Kodera, James. "Beyond Agreeing to Disagree - A Future Direction in Interfaith Dialogue." In *Interreligious Dialogue: Voices from a New Frontier*, ed. M. Darrol Bryant and Frank Flinn, 151-161. New York: Paragon House, 1989.

Mitra, Kana. *Catholicism-Hinduism: Vedantic Investigation of Raimundo Panikkar's Attempt at Bridgebuilding.* New York: University Press of America, 1987.

Nelson, Benjamin. "A New Science of Civilizational Analysis: A Tribute to Panikkar." *Cross Currents* 29 (Summer 1979): 135-140.

Podgorski, Frank. "Toward the Convergence of Religious Experience." *Cross Currents* 29 (Summer 1979): 231- 236.

Reetz, Dankfried. "Raymond Panikkar's Theology of Religions." *Religion and Society* 15 (1968): 32-54.

Schwöbel, Christoph. "Particularity, Universality, and the Religions." In *Christian Uniqueness Reconsidered*, ed. Gavin D'Costa, 30-46. Maryknoll: Orbis Books, 1990.

Slater, Peter. "Hindu and Christian Symbols in the Work of R. Panikkar." *Cross Currents* 29 (Summer 1979): 169-182.

Smet, Robert. *Dieu et l'homme. Contribution de Raymundo Panikkar au dialogue entre le Christianisme et l'hindouisme.* Doctoral dissertation, Université Catholique de Louvain, Belgium. Presented September, 1980. Publication listed with Ministry of External Affairs, Belgium.

_____. *Essai sur la pensée de Raimundo Panikkar: Une contribution indienne à la théologie des religions et à la christologie.* Louvain - la - Neuve: Centre d'histoire des religions, 1981.

_____. *Le problème d'une théologie hindoue-chrétienne selon Raymond Panikkar.* Louvain - la - Neuve: Centre d'histoire des religions, 1983.

Strolz, Walter. "Panikkar's Encounter with Hinduism." In *Dialogue and Syncretism*, ed. Jerald Gort, Hendrick Vroom, Rein Fernhout, and Anton Wessels, 146-152. Grand Rapids: William B. Eerdmans, 1989.

Thomas, M.M. "Foreword" to *The Trinity and World Religions. Icon-Person-Mystery*, Raymond Panikkar, v-ix. Madras: Christian Literature Society, 1970.

Williams, Rowan. "Trinity and Pluralism." In *Christian Uniqueness Reconsidered*, ed. Gavin D'Costa, 3-14. Maryknoll: Orbis Books, 1990.

Veliath, Dominic. *The Theological Approach and Understanding of Religions: Jean Daniélou and Raimundo Panikkar. A Study in Contrast.* Bangalore: Kristu Jyoti College, 1988.

Books on Related Topics

Abhishiktananda (Le Saux, Henri). *The Further Shore.* Delhi: I.S.P.C.K., 1975.

_____. *Guru and Disciple.* London: S.P.C.K., 1974.

_____. *Hindu-Christian Meeting Point.* Delhi: I.S.P.C.K., 1976.

_____. *The Mountain of the Lord.* Madras: C.L.S., 1966.

_____. *Prayer.* Delhi: I.S.P.C.K., 1975.

_____. *Saccidananda: A Christian Approach to Advaitic Experience.* Delhi: I.S.P.C.K., 1974.

_____. *Towards the Renewal of the Indian Church.* Bangalore: Dharmaram College, 1979.

Abraham, K.C., ed. *Third World Theologies: Commonalities and Divergences.* Maryknoll: Orbis Books, 1990.

Aurobindo, Sri. *Isha Upanishad.* Pondicherry: Sri Aurobindo Ashram, 1965.

Bracken, Joseph. *What Are They Saying About The Trinity?* New York: Paulist Press, 1979.

Bryant, M. Darrol and Frank Flinn, eds. *Interreligious Dialogue: Voices From a New Frontier.* New York: Paragon House, 1989.

Bühlmann, Walbert. *The Coming of the Third Church.* Maryknoll: Orbis Books, 1978.

_____. *God's Chosen People.* Maryknoll: Orbis Books, 1983.

Camps, Arnulf. *Partners in Dialogue: Christianity and Other World Reilgions.* New York: Orbis Books, 1983.

Carr, Edward H. *What is History?* New York: Random House, 1961.

Cobb, John. *Beyond Dialogue: Toward a Mutual Transformation of Christianity and Buddhism.* Philadelphia: Fortress Press, 1982.

Congar, Yves. *Je Crois en l'Espirit Saint. III: Le Fleuve de Vie coule en Orient et en Occident.* Paris: Les Éditions du Cérf, 1980.

Corless, Roger and Paul F. Knitter, eds. *Buddhist Emptiness and Christian Trinity.* New York: Paulist Press, 1990.

Coward, Harold. *Pluralism: Challenge to World Religions.* Maryknoll: Orbis Books, 1985.

Crowe, Frederick. *Son of God, Holy Spirit, and World Religions: The Contribution of Bernard Lonergan to the Wider Ecumenism.* Toronto: Regis College Press, 1985.

D'Costa, Gavin, ed. *Christian Uniqueness Reconsidered: The Myth of a Pluralistic Theology of Religions.* Maryknoll: Orbis Books, 1990.

Deussen, Paul. *The Philosophy of The Upanisads.* New York: Dover Publications, 1966.

_____. *The Philosophy of the Vedanta.* Calcutta: S. Gupta, 1957.

Deutsch, Eliot. *Advaita Vedanta: A Philosophical Reconstruction.* Honolulu: University of Hawaii Press, 1985.

Deutsch, Eliot and I.A.B. Van Buitenen, eds. *A Source Book of Advaita Vedanta.* Honolulu: University of Hawaii Press, 1971.

Dhavamony, Mariausai. *Classical Hinduism.* Rome: Università Gregoriana Editrice, 1982.

Dulles, Avery. *Models of Revelation.* Garden City: Doubleday, 1983.

Dunne, John S. *The Way of All the Earth: Experiments in Truth and Religion.* New York: Macmillan Press, 1972.

Dupuis, Jacques. *Jesus Christ at the Encounter of World Religions*, trans. Robert R. Barr. Maryknoll: Orbis Books, 1991.

Elenjimittam, Anthony, trans. *The Upanisads.* Bombay: Anthony Aquinas Publications, 1977.

Ernst, Cornelius. *Multiple Echo.* London: Darton, Longman and Todd, 1979.

Fabella, Virginia and Sergio Torres, eds. *Doing Theology in a Divided World.* Maryknoll: Orbis Books, 1985.

_____. *Irruption of the Third World.* Maryknoll: Orbis Books, 1983.

Fu, C. Wei-hsun and G.E. Spiegler, eds. *Religious Issues and Interreligious Dialogues.* New York: Greenwood Press, 1989.

Griffiths, Paul John. *Indian Buddhist Meditation Theory: His Story, Development and Systematization.* Ann Arbor: University Microfilms International, 1985.

Hick, John and Paul Knitter, eds. *The Myth of Christian Uniqueness.* Maryknoll: Orbis Books, 1989.

Hill, William J. *The Three-Personed God: The Trinity as a Mystery of Salvation.* Washington, D.C.: Catholic University of America Press, 1982.

Hughes, Edward I. *Wilfred Cantwell Smith: A Theology for the World.* London: SCM Press, 1986.

Idel, Moshe and Bernard McGinn, eds. *Mystic Union and Monotheistic Faith: An Ecumenical Dialogue*. New York: Macmillan Publishing Co., 1989.

John Paul II. *The Mission of Christ the Redeemer. Encyclical Letter. Redemptoris Missio* (Dec. 7, 1990), Vatican translation, Sherbrooke, Quebec: Éditions Paulines, 1991. *Acta Apostolicae Sedis* 83 (1991), 249-340.

Johnson, Elizabeth. *Consider Jesus: Waves of Renewal in Christology*. New York: Crossword, 1990.

Jüngel, Eberhart. *The Doctrine of the Trinity. God's Being is in Becoming*. Grand Rapids: Eerdmans, 1976.

Kaufman, Gordon. *Systematic Theology: A Historicist Perspective*. New York: Charles Scribner's Sons, 1968.

Kavanagh, Aidan. *On Liturgical Theology*. New York: Pueblo, 1984.

Keenan, John. *The Meaning of Christ*. Maryknoll: Orbis Books, 1989.

Kelly, Anthony. *The Trinity of Love: A Theology of the Christian God*. Delaware: Michael Glazier, 1989.

Knitter, Paul. *No Other Name? A Critical Survey of Christian Attitudes toward the World Religions*. Maryknoll: Orbis Books, 1985.

_____. ed. *Pluralism and Oppression: Theology in World Perspective*. New York: University Press of America, 1988.

_____. *Toward a Protestant Theology of Religions*. Marburg: N.G. Elwert, 1974.

Krieger, David J. *The New Universalism: Foundations for a Global Theology*. Maryknoll: Orbis Books, 1991.

Küng, Hans and Jürgen Moltmann, eds. *Christianity Among World Religions*. Edinburg: T. & T. Clark, 1986.

La Cugna, Catherine Mowry. *God For Us: The Trinity and Christian Life*. San Francisco: Harper, 1973.

Lane, Dermot. *The Reality of Jesus*. New York: Paulist Press, 1975.

Lockhead, David. *The Dialogical Imperative: A Christian Reflection on Interfaith Encounter*. Maryknoll: Orbis Books, 1988.

Lonergan, Bernard. *Insight*. New York: Philosophical Library, 1970.

_____. *Method in Theology*. New York: Herder and Herder, 1972.

_____. *Philosophy of God and Theology*. Philadelphia: Westminster Press, 1973.

_____. *The Way to Nicea*. Philadelphia: Westminster Press, 1976.

Macquarrie, John. *Principles of Christian Theology*. 2nd ed., New York: Charles Scribner's Sons, 1977.

Masters, Donald C. *The Christian Idea of History*. Waterloo: Waterloo Lutheran University, 1962.

Mattam, Joseph. *Catholic Approaches to Hinduism: A Study of the Work of the European Orientalists and R.C. Zaehner*. Delhi: Anand Press, 1974.

_____. *Land of Trinity: A Study of Modern Christian Approaches to Hinduism*. Bangalore: Theological Publications in India, 1975.

Mayeda, Sengaku, trans. *A Thousand Teachings: The Upadesasahasri of Sankara*. Tokyo: University of Tokyo Press, 1977.

Menacherry, Cheriyan. *An Indian Philosophical Approach to the Personality of Jesus Christ.* Rome: Urbaniana University Press, 1986.

Momigliano, Arnaldo. *The Classical Foundations of Modern Historiography.* Berkeley: University of California Press, 1990.

Morgan, Kenneth, ed. *The Religion of the Hindus.* New York: Ronald Press, 1953.

Muppathyil, Cyriac. *Meditation as a Path to God-Realization.* Rome: Gregorian University Press, 1979.

Murti, T.R.V. *The Central Philosophy of Buddhism.* London: George Allen and Unwin, 1960.

Neuner, Joseph, ed. *Christian Revelation and World Religions.* London: Burns & Oates, 1967.

Nichols, Aidan. *The Shape of Catholic Theology. An Introduction to Its Sources, Principles, and History.* Collegeville: Liturgical Press, 1991.

O'Flaherty, Wendy Doniger. *The Origins of Evil in Hindu Mythology.* Berkeley: University of California Press, 1976.

_____. *Other Peoples' Myths: The Cave of Echoes.* New York: Macmillan Publishing Co., 1988.

_____, ed. and trans. *The Rig Veda: An Anthology.* Middlesex: Penguin Books, 1981.

Oxtoby, Willard, *The Meaning of Other Faiths.* Philadelphia: Westminster Press, 1983.

Parrinder, G. *Avatar and Incarnation.* New York: Barnes and Noble, 1970.

Pereira, Jose, ed. *Hindu Theology.* Garden City: Image Books, 1976.

Prabhavananda, Swami. *The Spiritual Heritage of India.* Hollywood: Vedanta Press, 1963.

Prabhavananda, Swami and Christopher Isherwood, trans. *Shankara's Crest-Jewel of Discrimination (Viveka Chudamani) with A Garland of Questions and Answers.* New York: New American Library, 1970.

Prabhupada, Swami, trans. *Bhagavad-Gita As It Is.* New York: Collier Books, 1972.

Race, Alan. *Christians and Religious Pluralism. Patterns in the Christian Theology of Religions.* Maryknoll: Orbis Books, 1982.

Radhakrishnan, S., ed. *Contemporary Indian Philosophy.* London: George Allen and Unwin, 1953.

_____. *The Principal Upanisads.* London: George Allen & Unwin, 1953.

Rahner, Karl. *Theological Investigations IV. More Recent Writings,* trans. Kevin Smith. Baltimore: Helicon Press, 1969.

_____. *The Trinity,* trans. Joseph Donceel. New York: Herder and Herder, 1970.

Rahula, Wapola. *What the Buddha Taught.* New York: Grove Press, 1974.

Rajappan, Immanuel. *The Influence of Hinduism on Indian Christians.* Jabalpur: Leonard Theological College, 1950.

Ratzinger, Joseph. *The God of Jesus Christ: Meditations on God in the Trinity*, trans. Robert J. Cunningham. Chicago: Franciscan Herald Press, 1979.

Ratzinger, Cardinal Joseph with Vittorio Messori, *The Ratzinger Report.* San Francisco: Ignatius Press, 1985. (Translated by Salvator Attanasio and Graham Harrison).

Rousseau, Richard, ed. *Christianity and the Religions of the East.* Scranton: Ridge Row Press, 1982.

Samartha, S.J. *One Christ - Many Religions: Toward a Revised Christology.* Maryknoll: Orbis Books, 1991.

Scharlemann, Robert, ed. *Naming God.* New York: Paragon House, 1985.

Schner, G.P., ed. *The Documents of Vatican II Reconsidered.* New York: University Press of America, 1986.

Secretariatus Pro Non - Christianis. *The Attitude of the Church towards the Followers of Other Religions: Reflections and Orientations on Dialogue and Mission.* Ottawa: Canadian Conference of Catholic Bishops, Pentecost, 1984.

_____. *For a Dialogue with Hinduism.* Rome: Editrice Ancora, no date given. Collaborators: Cyril Papali, Mariasusai Dhavamony, Pierre Fallon and Paolo Marella.

Sen, Keshab Chandra. *Keshab Chandra Sen's Lectures in India.* London: Cassell, 1909.

Sharkey, Michael, ed. *International Theological Commission. Texts and Documents. 1969 - 1985*, San Francisco: Ignatius Press, 1989.

Sivaraman, Krishna, ed. *Hindu Spirituality: Vedas through Vedanta.* New York: Crossroad, 1989.

Sullivan, Francis A. *Magisterium. Teaching Authority in the Catholic Church.* New York: Paulist Press, 1983.

Thompson, William. *The Jesus Debate: A Survey and Synthesis.* New York: Paulist Press, 1985.

Thundy, Zacharias P., Kuncheria Pathid, Frank Podgorski, eds. *Religions in Dialogue: East and West Meet.* New York: University Press of America, 1985.

Tracy, David. *Dialogue with the Other: The Inter-Religious Dialogue.* Louvain: Peeters Press, 1991.

Vagaggini, Cyprian. *The Theological Dimensions of the Liturgy.* Collegeville: Liturgical Press, 1976.

Verdu, Alfonso. *The Philosophy of Buddhism.* Boston: Martinus Nijhoff Publishers, 1981.

Whaling, Frank, ed. *The World's Religious Traditions: Current Perspectives in Religious Studies.* New York: Crossword, 1986.

Whelan, Joseph, ed. *The God Experience.* New York: Newman Press, 1971.

Articles on Related Topics

Banerjea, Jitendra N. "The Hindu Concept of God." In *The Religion of the Hindus*, ed. Kenneth Morgan, 48-82. New York: Ronald Press, 1953.

Beeck, Frans Jozef van. "Professing the Uniqueness of Christ." *Chicago Studies* 24 (April 1985): 17-35.

Bilimoria, Purusottama. "Avatara: Descent of the Spirit." *Hinduism* 96 (1982): 4-11.

Carmody, Denise Lardner. "Review Symposium: Paul F. Knitter's *No Other Name? A Critical Survey of Christian Attitudes toward the World Religions*." *Horizons* 13 (Spring 1986): 122-123.

Coffy, Robert. "The Magisterium and Theology." *Irish Theological Quarterly* 43 (1976): 247-259.

Courtney, F. "Cano, Melchior." *New Catholic Encyclopedia* 3 (1967): 28-29.

Crawford, Cromwell. "The Buddha's Thoughts on Thinking: Implications for Ecumenical Dialogue." *Journal of Ecumenical Studies* 21 (Spring 1984): 229-247.

Crowe, Frederick. "The Inner Word of the Spirit." In *Theology of the Christian Word*. Toronto: Paulist Press, 1978.

_____. "Son and Spirit: Tension in the Divine Missions?" *Lonergan Workshop* (1983): 1-21.

D'Souza, Mervyn. "Krishna and Arjuna: A Model of Guru-Sishya Relationship." *Journal of Dharma* 11 (Jan.- March 1986): 9-16.

Dulles, Avery. "Faith and Revelation." In *Systematic Theology. Roman Catholic Perspectives*. Vol. I, ed. F.S. Fiorenza and J.P. Galvin, 91-128. Minneapolis: Fortress Press, 1991.

Hanvey, James. "The Incarnation, the Cross and Spirituality." *The Way* 25 (July 1985): 206-223.

Happel, Stephen. "Theologian." *New Catholic Encyclopedia*, 17 (1979): 649-651.

Hirudayam, Ignatius. "My Spiritual Journey Through the Highways and Byways of Interreligous Dialogue." In *Interreligous Dialogue: Services From a New Frontier*, ed. M.D. Bryant and F. Flinn, 53-63. New York: Paragon House, 1989.

John Paul II. "Dialogue to Love." *The Pope Speaks* 31 (Summer 1986): 133-137. *Acta Apostolicae Sedis* 78 (1986): 766-771.

Kariamadam, Paul. "India and Luke's Theology of the Way." *Bible Bhashyam* 11 (March-June 1985): 47-60.

Kiesling, Christopher. "On Relating to the Persons of the Trinity." *Theological Studies* 47 (1986): 599-616.

Knitter, Paul. "Anonymous Christianity and the Missions." *Verbum* 10 (1968): 402-405.

_____. "Roman Catholic Approaches to Other Religions: Developments and Tensions." *International Bulletin of Missionary Research* 8 (April 1984): 50-54.

_____. "The Wider Ecumenism: Exploring New Directions." *Ecumenical Trends* 15 (Sept. 1986): 134-137.

La Cugna, Catherine. "Seminar on the Trinity." In *Proceedings of the Catholic Theological Society of America* 39 (1984): 192-195.

_____. "Seminar on the Trinity." In *Proceedings of the Catholic Theological Society of America* 40 (1985): 191-193.

Laughlin, M.F. "Joachim of Fiore." *New Catholic Encyclopedia* 7 (1967): 990-991.

Mattam, Joseph. "Dialogue and Incarnation." In *Land of the Trinity*. Bangalore: Theological Publications in India, 1975.

McDonnell, Kilian. "A Trinitarian Theology of the Holy Spirit?" *Theological Studies* 46 (1985): 191-227.

Moffit, John. "Christianity Confronts Hinduism." *Theological Studies* 30 (1969): 207 - 224.

Mohammed, Ovey. "Commentary on the Declaration on the Relationship of the Church to Non-Christian Religions, *Nostra Aetate.*" In *The Church Renewed: The Documents of Vatican II Reconsidered*, ed. G.P. Schner, 135-142. New York: University Press of America, 1986.

O'Carroll, Michael. "Appropriation." *Trinitas. A Theological Encyclopedia of the Holy Trinity* (1987): 17.

Organ, Troy. "Some Contributions of Hinduism to Christianity." In *Christianity and the Religions of the East*, ed. Richard Rousseau, Scranton: Ridge Row Press, 1982.

Paul VI. *Address* to those participating in the Symposium of African Bishops at Kampala, July 31, 1969. *Acta Apostolicae Sedis* 61 (1969), 573-578.

Rahner, Karl. "Towards a Fundamental Theological Interpretation of Vatican II." *Theological Studies* 40 (1979): 716-727.

Rahner, Karl and Herbert Vorgrimler. "Appropriation," *Dictionary of Theology* (1981): 26.

Sahadat, John. "The Interreligious Study of Mysticism and a Sense of Universality." *Journal of Ecumenical Studies* 22 (Spring 1985): 292-311.

Semmelroth, Otto and Karl Lehmann. "Commentary on the Theses." In *Readings in Moral Theology No. 3: The Magisterium and Morality*, ed. C.E. Curran and R.A. McCormick, 160-170. New York: Paulist Press, 1982.

Sundararajan, K.R. "The Hindu Models of Interreligious Dialogue." *Journal of Ecumenical Studies* 23 (Spring 1986): 239-250.

Thomas, M.M. "Christology and Pluralistic Consciousness." *International Bulletin* 10 (July 1986): 106-108.

Whaling, Frank. "The Trinity and Structure of Religious Life." In *Christianity and the Religions of the East*, ed. Richard Rousseau, 43-51. Scranton: Ridge Row Press, 1982.

III. General Works Cited

Acta Apostolicae Sedis. Commentarium Officiale. Vatican City: *Typis Polyglottis Vaticanis.* Vol. 1 (1909) - Vol. 84 (1992).

A Concise Dictionary of Theology. Gerald O'Collins and Edward Farrugia. New York: Paulist Press, 1991.

Dictionary of Theology, 2nd ed. Karl Rahner and Herbert Vorgrimler. Trans. by Richard Strachan et al. New York: Crossroad, 1981.

The Documents of Vatican II. In A New and Definitive Translation with Commentaries and Notes by Catholic, Protestant and Orthodox Authorities, ed. Walter M. Abbott. New York: Herder and Herder, 1966.

Enchiridion Symbolorum, Definitionum et Declarationum de rebus fidei et morum. Ed. Henricus Denzinger and Adolphus Schönmetzer. 36th ed. Freiburg im Br.: Herder, 1976.

The Holy Bible. New Revised Standard Version. Oxford: Oxford University Press, 1989.

New Catholic Encyclopedia. Ed.-in-Chief, William J. MacDonald. Catholic University of America, Washington, D.C., 18 volumes: 1-15 (1967); 16 (1974); 17 (1979); 18 (1989).

The Sacred Books of the East. Ed. F. Max Müller. Trans. by various Oriental scholars. Delhi: Motilal Banarsidass, 1965. University Press, 1882.

Trinitas. A Theological Encyclopedia of The Holy Trinity. Michael O'Carroll. Wilmington: Michael Glazier, 1987.

The Upanishads. Trans. Swami Nikhilananda. New York: Harper Torchbooks, 1963.